Draw Me

The Deep Cry of the Bride

Steve Porter

Draw Me - The Deep Cry of the Bride

Copyright © 2018 Steve Porter

All Rights Reserved. No part of this publication may be reproduced, stored in a retrieval system or transmitted in any form or by any means – electronic, mechanical, photocopy, recording or any other – except for brief quotations in printed reviews, without the

prior permission of the author.

All Scripture quotations, unless otherwise specified, are from the King James Version of the Bible (Copyright © 1977, 1984, Thomas Nelson Inc., Publishers.)

Scriptures marked NIV are from the New International Version of the Bible (Copyright © 1973, 1978, 1984, International Bible Society. Used by permission of Zondervan Bible Publishers. All rights reserved.)

ISBN-13: 978-1984993274

Dedicated to my fellow classmates of Pinecrest Bible Training Center, Salisbury Center, NY

"Draw me, we will run after thee: the king hath brought me into his chambers: we will be glad and rejoice in thee, we will remember thy love more than wine: the upright love thee" (Song of Solomon 1:4).

"Deep calls unto deep at the noise of your waterfalls: all your waves and your billows are gone over me" (Psalms 42:7).

For I hear the Lord whisper, "for even the greatest hunger that you have possessed in your past will only be the starting point of the hunger that I will give you. For I am placing a great hunger in the heart of My Bride and she will not be content with 'things' but only my 'face'... I am calling you deeper today," says the Lord! "Will you cry out to me with all your heart?"

Acknowledgments

Thank you to my lovely sweet wife, Diane, my loving father and mother, Wayne & Elizabeth Porter, and my beautiful girls, Alyssa Porter Hudson & Britney Porter, for their support of my writing.

Thank you to the late Wade Taylor, my spiritual father of twenty-three years who imparted so much into my life leading up into his graduation to Heaven. Thank you to the late Walter Beuttler, late Hattie Hammond, and the late John Wright Follette for inspiring me with their ministries more than they will ever know.

Thanks as well to Nancy Taylor Warner, Bishop Frank Dupree, and Pastor Jay Francis for their friendship and positive influence in my life.

I would like to thank my editors, Nancy Arant Williams and Ken Darrow, for their excellent and anointed editing skills.

Lastly and most importantly, I thank my beautiful Savior who whispered these truths into my ear. Thank you for wooing me, never giving up on me, and loving me with an everlasting love!

TABLE OF CONTENTS

Acknowledgments v

Foreword...ix

Introduction 1

Prologue 3

Chapter 1: Into His Chambers 7

Chapter 2: When the Bride Finds Favor with Her Groom 23

Chapter 3: The Cry to Go Deeper 31

Chapter 4: A Holy Desperation 39

Chapter 5: The Bride Who Presses In 47

Chapter 6: The King's College 59

Chapter 7: One Glance from His Eyes......................... 67

Chapter 8: His Bride Has Dove Eyes 79

Chapter 9: Rise up and Come Away 89

Chapter 10: Forgetting Those Things That

Are Behind 93

Chapter 11: Deep Healing and God's Secrets 111

Chapter 12: He Cometh Leaping upon the Mountains 115

Chapter 13: He Announced His Presence 121

Chapter 14: A Bride That Prepares........................... 131

Chapter 15: The Preparation of a Queen 137

Chapter 16: The War Within 141

Chapter 17: Purification of the Bride........................ 145

Chapter 18: The Favor of God That Rests 153

Chapter 19: The Shepherd's Tent 157

Chapter 20: The Lantern Left by Wade Taylor 161

Chapter 21: My Company of Overcomers 167

Chapter 22: The Upward Call..................................... 175

Chapter 23: The Bridegroom Takes Us by the Hands 183

About the Author 189

Foreword

By Michael Fickess
Teacher and Author at Morningstar Ministries

The first time I met Steve Porter, we had only a brief introduction at a small local church. However, I was struck by the beauty and power of what He carried. As someone who operates in prophetic discernment, I could see a beautiful white light shining from his face throughout the worship service. But what I *felt* went much deeper than what I *saw*, for as I looked at the white glow around his face, I could feel his abandoned love for God and his passion to prepare the Bride of Christ. The manifest presence of the Lord that Steve carried reminded me distinctly of Wade Taylor. Now, I have learned these simple impressions were no accident—for Wade Taylor was a primary influence in Steve's life and ministry.

I share this story because there is big difference between an *ordinary* Christian book and an *authentic message* from the Lord. Anyone can write an ordinary Christian book that expounds on their favorite scriptures or gives basic encouragement and inspiration. However, it takes a special person to record a transformative message from the very heart of God. While an ordinary book can give some inspiration for a short season, the prophetic message of this book has the power to transform and impact the reader in much deeper and lasting ways.

There are many streams—or movements—in the Body of Christ and each one has a purpose. Some of these streams have swept through the whole Body of Christ already, while others have remained small and hidden away until their appointed time. The stream of God that began with Wade Taylor's remarkable relationship with God and rich teaching has been hidden away for a long time, awaiting its appointed season to flow through the Body of Christ. This is a special stream that is laden with hunger for God, a balance of Word and Spirit, and the call to live a lifestyle of consecration, abandoned love, and holiness. I think the Lord has kept this stream hidden for a long time to protect it, but we are now entering the season where the whole Body of Christ will need it. As I read this book, it became clear to me that Steve has become one of the stewards of this special stream and we are about to enter the appointed time when it flow down from the rocky crags and pine trees, to wash over the Bride and **"make her ready" (Revelation 19:7).**

After Elijah was tormented by Jezebel's curse, he fled to Mount Horeb to hear from God. On his way up the mountain to hear from God, Elijah passed fires, winds, and earthquakes that God **"was not in" (1 Kings**

19:11). When he finally reached the cave at the summit, he wrapped his face in his mantle to shut out every distraction and hear the **"still, small voice of God"** with clarity **(1 Kings 19:12).** In order to get the full benefit of this book, I recommend shutting out all distractions and welcoming the Holy Spirit to touch and open your heart to the beautiful message in this book. There are many messages that may bring fire, wind, or shaking—but this whispered message from the heart of God may be more timely and urgent than all of them.

**Shalom,
Michael Fickess**

Introduction

Welcome. I've been waiting for you. You didn't stumble upon this book by chance but by divine appointment, which has been my prayer as I wrote this message. I asked God to do something very special as you read, so that your life would be forever transformed. I didn't rush the process but allowed the Spirit of God to download His message into my heart over a period of several years, knowing that it's a living love letter for Christ's Bride.

If you're touched while reading it's not because of me, because I'm just a man; rather it's because Christ is giving you a personal revelation of Himself and allowing you to feel His manifest presence so that you'll never be the same again. At that point you'll be face to face, looking into the very eyes of Love itself. I pray that, later on, you will think back fondly to the night when Jesus came and touched you. Let me pray before we get started.

Father, in the name of Jesus I thank you for this dear reader. I thank you for this special opportunity to come and minister. I ask that the Holy Spirit would step in, and move, as I simply become a yielded vessel. I ask that you impart the anointed word of our loving Lord. Let your Word come forth with unction and clarity to every person who reads it. Back it up, Lord, with your presence and power, changing them as they discover who you are and how much you really love them. Hide me behind your cross so that you receive all the glory in Jesus' name. Amen!

I want to encourage you to push aside whatever you're facing today because when you're close to receiving a revelation from Jesus, the enemy will inevitably come to snatch it away, if you let him. He will invade the atmosphere with every kind of distraction, hoping you leave it to collect dust on a shelf and never pick it up again. Instead cover yourself with the shield of faith, lift up the sword of the Spirit and say, "Satan, you're not going to steal this treasure. You're not going to hinder what God wants to do in my life."

I believe that Jesus wants to take over as you read. So regardless of what's happening today you just shake it off and determine not to allow any hindrances, saying, "I'm going to give it my full and complete attention, and let the Lord have His way in my life." I'm praying that, as you read, you'll be changed, healed, delivered and walk into deeper intimacy with the Lord. To you who fit that description, I say, "Keep reading. Your answer is on the way!"

Prologue

This book was motivated by a deep desire for the church to come up higher. If you desire to go higher in your walk with God, you'll love this revelation, but it's not for the faint of heart or for those seeking a cheap and easy, instant Christianity. God is calling His people to a higher level of intimacy, where they are changed as they enter into and abide in His manifest presence.

At this point I need to make it clear that we can never save ourselves or earn God's love no matter how many good works we do. Salvation is only delivered by grace, through faith in the finished work of Christ.

"For it is by grace you have been saved, through faith—and this is not from yourselves, it is the gift of God"— (Eph. 2:8).

We come to Christ just as we are, weak and wayward, but we're made righteous and clean through the work of the cross as we repent and trust in Christ, not only to save us but to train and change our very character at its essence so that we actually resemble Him, which means we are never our own again. **(Ye are not your**

own, but are bought with a price, (1 Cor. 6:20) **the precious blood of Jesus.)** As we grow, our desires should reflect that growth so that we leave behind the old, dead things and seek to please God in all we say and do.

As mature believers it's then our responsibility to continually examine ourselves to guard against falling away and leaving behind our first love. In this process, we have to say, "Show me, Lord, where I need to change. Then change me by the power of your Spirit because I can't change without you." At that point, we simply rest in His abiding, moment-by-moment presence, studying His Word and allowing the Holy Spirit to transform us. As we do these things we'll never be the same again and will have no use for the way things were. We're being continually transformed at our core level, which is exactly what God intended.

While salvation is a free gift, it's up to us to respond to the wooing of the Holy Spirit, seeking God, digging into the Word, developing a passion for Him and for souls, in order to live out our destiny on the Earth. Ultimately, because the flesh will always resist as we submit to God's will, we must carefully guard our treasure, knowing we have it all—in Jesus, the Pearl of greatest price.

In the end, it's all about Him and how much we love, adore and serve Him with all our hearts, souls, minds, and strength, willing and ready to step out to win the lost while there's still time and do even greater things than Jesus did. Even as Walter Beuttler (we will talk more about him later) has said many times, **"When you build God a house of devotion He will build you that house of ministry."** Everything flows out of pure devotion as unto the Lord. Read on.

CHAPTER 1

Into His Chambers

Right now, the lukewarm, apathetic spirit of Laodicea is doing its best to blind the eyes of the Body of Christ, while the Lord is busy preparing a pure and beautiful Bride for His Son. The Bride is 'buying gold tried by fire'—His divine nature. In His presence our nature is transformed so that we become that radiant Bride that shines with the very glory of our God.

My deepest desire is that we know Christ on a deep, abiding level and are full of God's treasure—that we would have a personal revelation from a personal Christ. If we're going to be changed and become His Bride it won't be because of our accomplishments; it will be because we're desperate for our Bridegroom when we're willing to say, "I'm ready to stay on my face, stay on my knees, fasting and praying, as long as it takes, contending with Heaven, eager and ready to see Him face to face, in the here and now."

I often travel to churches where Christians are clearly content with the status quo. It's as if they're saying, "I don't need anything more. I'm happy with the way things are. Happy that I'm saved, baptized, filled with the Holy Spirit and speak in tongues." They have no idea that Father wants us to work in harmony with His Spirit, to do even greater things than Jesus did, to transform the world. It's like a spirit of apathy has mesmerized the church and put it to sleep, robbing us of our inheritance and the impetus to bring in the harvest before Jesus returns.

Yet I get excited when I see some who are hungry for more. This remnant is saying, "There has to be more than a sermon with three points and a poem followed by a song and closing prayer." And they're right. There must be hunger, where desperate people seek more of God and won't take no for an answer. I believe the Lord wants to impart that kind of fresh hunger, so I'm asking, **"Lord, would you increase our hunger right now? In this world with all its distractions, would you make us desperate for more of you, unwilling to settle for less?"**

The Song of Solomon inspires a deeper hunger for God. It prepares the church to be His mature Bride.

The Song Above Every Song!

In Chapter one, verse one it says,

"The song of songs which is Solomon's" (v.1).

Solomon wrote over a thousand songs, yet he describes this one as *The Song of Songs*. In other words, he's saying, "This is the greatest song I've ever written." And if that's the case, it wasn't written by accident; it was done by divine appointment—anointed.

I've often heard others teach on this book; some portray it as a surface book that illustrates human love between a husband and wife. I've also heard some say that it symbolizes just the love between Solomon and the Shulamite woman. But I would prefer to see Solomon as a type of Jesus Christ and the Shulamite as a type of the Bride of Christ in training who deeply desires her Bridegroom. Make no bones about it, the Song of Solomon is truly a present word!

In Chapter one verse 2 it says,

"Let Him kiss me with the kisses of his mouth, for thy love is better than wine."

Notice that she repeats that word "kiss" again for emphasis. Here we see the Shulamite woman who desired far more than a casual pat on the arm. She wanted a kiss from the king. She wanted to show him how much she loved him and was eager to embrace and kiss him to prove it. In order to kiss someone you have to get close . . . face to face—to lean in and connect with that person. Our Heavenly Bridegroom wants a Bride that is eager to be face to face with Him—to lean in and connect heart to heart.

I love the term "the kiss of His presence"; let me explain. Over the last twenty-five years, the Lord has been teaching me what it means to receive the "kiss of His presence." Over the years I've spent time alone in prayer, with worship playing in the background, while I saturated myself in the presence of the Lord, and it was like He actually stepped into the room. His presence was truly there; it was so powerful that I was deeply touched and couldn't help but weep. What exactly was happening? I was receiving a **kiss of His presence.** His manifest presence was right there. I didn't have to wonder where He was. At that instant I felt Him beside me. Now we know that Jesus is omnipresent, that is everywhere at one time—this is called His abiding presence. But it's something entirely different and much more intimate to have His manifest presence step down from Heaven to the place where we are.

In that moment when we were spending time together, He gave me the kiss of His presence. In fact, you can be alone in the middle of a church service and receive a kiss of His presence, where you know you've had a face-to-face encounter with Him. It can even happen in your car. At times I've been driving, not even thinking about the Lord, when His presence suddenly filled the car. This is why I call my car "The Glory Car" because the Lord often visits me in my car! When it comes to His presence, I'm a cry baby—I can't help it. Some people say, "Men shouldn't cry," but I'm telling you that when you're in the presence of a loving Father, you can't help but cry. How can you not weep when you sense the depth of His love, feeling His nearness, when He suddenly becomes so real to you?

I teach on this all the time—how we must take Jesus off the painting on the wall, off mere words in a book. We need to make Him real and personal. We're transformed when He becomes personal—when His exquisitely loving presence walks in to embrace and kiss us. When we yearn for more, seeking more of our Heavenly Bridegroom, He reveals Himself to us in our prayer rooms, our cars or even while we're taking a walk. I'm not talking about just an emotional high here. I'm talking about Jesus, the Son of God, manifesting Himself in the place where we are.

Walks with God

One day, when I was taking a walk on Lake Erie in Northeast Ohio, where I used to go to the beach especially to pray for Canada while watching the sunset, it was as if Jesus stood beside me, so we could watch it together. He was as real as you and I. This was not my first walk with him on that beach as I often walked the shore barefoot, talking with Him in close communion. That day he showed me that He deeply desires to be that real to us, and not just on rare occasions. It should be a common occurrence.

Let me take a moment to declare even as you read this, "Lord, kiss me with the kisses of your mouth, for your love is better than wine." How can we compare that kind of love to any other? We can't. It's like comparing apples with oranges. I'm not giving you a new revelation you've never heard before. Rather, my goal is to stir a deep hunger for His presence in your life. In fact, I pray that, when you finish this book, you don't say, "Wow! What a great writer Steve is. He really knows his complicated Bible dictionary." No, I want you to finish this book, saying, "Wow! I feel a deeper hunger for The Master than I've ever felt in my life." My prayer is for you to want to go find a quiet place to be alone with your Bridegroom where you can shut the door and get down on your face to seek Him and not take no for an answer.

At times we've had people listen or watch our messages on our website and report back that they've had encounters with the Holy Spirit as they listened, and that deeply touches us. Today, my prayer is that, no matter what device you're using to read this book, you'll be stirred, eager for the kiss of His presence. When that happens, He will also quicken scripture to you. Have you ever read something many times over, like, "Let Him kiss me with the kisses of His mouth," and it meant nothing to you but then suddenly you're reading scripture and it's quickened, coming alive, and stirs the embers of passion into an unquenchable flame in your heart?

This is another type of "kiss of His presence," when He gives you an unexpected revelation while reading scripture. It's as if the Rhema words of God become *alive* as never before. It's no longer just a Logos (a written word only); it's Rhema; it's on fire and all of a sudden you see some truth you've never seen before. What is that? That's the kiss of His presence. It's when His very presence comes and begins to whisper in your ear, to teach you a precious truth you've never understood before, and from that moment on, you carry that truth as your own new present reality.

I had many seasons with the Lord over the years when He would have me praying all night long. I would have my Bible in my lap, and as I was praying I was underlining and circling things that were coming alive for the very first time. And because of the kiss of His presence in the night in the King's College, I have understood and now teach as truth what came alive to me during those times.

As I was praying He would reveal a powerful truth and I would gladly make it my own. In reality, once you receive a personal revelation, or Rhema truth from God, you'll never forget it. It's like a precious gift from Father that's then tucked into your heart that you'll speak without prompting at the exact moment you need it. Why does that happen? It happens because the Lord gave you the kiss of His presence and imparted a truth that's alive and on fire. This kind of truth isn't mere information; it's the kind of truth that changes a congregation and changes a culture. It must be quickened; it must be the result of the kiss of His presence.

Thy Name Is as Ointment Poured Forth

In verse 3 we read:

"Because of the savour of thy good ointments thy name is as ointment poured forth, therefore do the virgins love thee."

Consider the phrase: "Thy name is as ointment poured forth." There is a special anointing on the name of Jesus. Now, when I say my own name—Steve—nothing happens. The same thing happens when I say, "In the name of Mark be healed." As lovely as that name Mark is, no one's going to get healed by that name, but when someone says the name of Jesus in faith with power and presence, they will be healed—they will be changed!

We can usually tell how much He really means to them when we hear them say His name. Have you ever heard an unbeliever pray something like this: "Oh God, up there in Heaven, we thank you for your blessing, God," and you just know Jesus is a distant stranger to them? Then suddenly someone else prays and they say His name, "Jesus!" And when they say His name it's not the voice inflection, it's not how much emotion they put into saying the name, but there's something really alive there...a under current so to speak. They're in love with Jesus; you know it when they say His name!

Remember back when you were dating and you said that special name—it meant something to you, your heart was leaping when you were dating; the same thing happens with Jesus. "Jesus." His name is like "ointment poured forth, therefore do the virgins love thee."

For instance, I love listening to the sermons of a famous old-time evangelist named Hattie Hammond. We will talk more about her later. Often, when she began her sermon, she said the name of Jesus over and over. Oh, how electricity fills the room as she says His name—Jesus—even on tape or CD! It's clear that she knew Jesus personally because the ointment poured forth as she called on His name.

As we say His name, "Jesus," it releases the anointing into the atmosphere in a service. I've been in services when I didn't even get a chance to preach, we just said His name, "Jesus." And at that moment a powerful anointing was released into the room. His name is not the name of a stranger but of a dear and intimate friend.

Draw Me!

I covered all those verses to focus on the key verse of this book—verse 4 where it says:

"Draw me, we will run after thee, the King has brought me into his chambers."

This verse has three parts. Part one says, "Draw me." Part two, "we will run after thee." Part three, "the king has brought me into his chambers." What did it mean when she cried out, "Draw me?"

I've spent hours, weeks, months, even years thinking about the phrase, "Draw me." It's the very cry of a smitten Bride's heart, desperately praying as one who is not content with the status quo, and cries out, "Draw me." Can you see this happening right now in the body of Christ? In remnant churches and gatherings, I can tell immediately that they're expectant—hungry for more than just religion—and they're crying out, "Draw me!" In other words, "Lord, make me more spiritually hungry than I was before. Place a deep hunger in me so that I no longer fall captive to the distractions of the enemy. Draw me closer." In other words, "Enlarge my capacity to be filled, and make me expectant for more, so that I won't settle for less than your best."

I often pray this prayer: "Lord, draw me. Increase my spiritual hunger." We can easily become content where we are, allowing ourselves to become apathetic so that we sit in church week after week, month after month, and leave without ever being changed. Yet there are some who are crying out, "Draw me, Lord, I'm thankful for what I have, but I want more—a deeper spiritual hunger than I've ever had before. Draw me, my Heavenly Bridegroom. Pull me closer to you, Precious One!"

At this very moment His deepest desire is to awaken a new hunger in us, wooing us to go deeper in relationship with Him. He's calling our names, saying, "Come." If you were to be quiet right now and listen, not with your natural ears but with your spirit, you'd hear the Spirit of God say, **"Come. I'm calling you away from ev-**

ery distraction. You've been pulled in the opposite direction from Me, and now I'm calling you back." Can you hear Him say, **"I'm already drawing you to Myself. My Dove, I'm already calling your name. I'm already wooing you—waiting for you to come"?**

When the Bridegroom draws us, we become desperate and run after Him, which speaks of a place of consecration where unnecessary and sinful things begin to lose their appeal and fall away from us. Does anybody besides me need a few things to fall away? Are you perfect? Perhaps you have certain areas of the flesh or some attitudes or mindsets that aren't under His lordship and the Lord is saying, "Run hard after Me, and in the process, I'm going to get rid of what needs to go."

When He does that, our attitudes will change; our mindsets will change, and our old scars will be healed. As a result, there will be a new and deeper level of consecration and commitment when God says, "Son, daughter run hard after Me, pursue Me, chase Me because in the process you'll be changed into My image." A metamorphosis happens at this point, producing a change, a transformation. I often feel that I'm not worthy to be near Him because I'm flawed, and yet, when I feel that way, He draws me to Himself. But even in the middle of this kind of pursuit, the enemy is going to say, "You'll never change." In this place, it's easy to be disappointed by our lack of growth. But when a friend sees us after a long absence, they are going to say, "Wow, they have changed! I hardly recognize them!"

It's important to remember that our growth can't be measured with a yardstick. So trust God, and know that He's in control of the timing if we simply seek Him with all that's in us. When we rush God's hands to move faster, we quickly begin to see that His pace is the only one we can handle. **We grow inch by inch, not mile by mile, that we may be that Oak tree of righteousness, firmly rooted in Him.**

The Devil is always busy when we're praying. When we're seeking Abba, soaking in His presence, usually about forty-five minutes into the process, the enemy will whisper, "You're wasting your time." You know you're not wasting your time, but at that point you're wondering why nothing is happening. You know His presence is there, but you're not feeling anything and you think, *Maybe I'm wasting my time.* But don't believe that lie from Satan because, even as you stay and hold your course, you will allow your heart to run after Him.

In that time of pursuit you're being changed and growing whether you see it or not. Isn't that amazing? **No time spent in His presence is *ever* wasted.** The truth is that it's a very wise investment. Just think of it this way: **every time you bask in His presence, you're investing your time—every time!**

Sneaking Away with the Lord

When I'm at home I often sneak away to be alone with Father. Several years ago, when my girls were younger, I thought I was all alone in praise and worship, when I was suddenly in His presence. I looked over and saw my daughter Alyssa standing there. His presence was overwhelming, and I knew that I was being changed. But not only was I being changed, my daughter was being changed because, when you persevere, not only will you be changed, but it will spill over and change the lives of those around you. My heart just melted when I saw her raising her hands in sweet worship and adoration before HER Lord!

The phrase, "Draw me," speaks of a far deeper spiritual hunger, and the phrase, "We will run after thee," speaks of consecration. Now let's get to the good part where the King welcomes us into His chambers! The word "chamber" speaks of intimacy. It was only under the threat of death that someone entered an Old Testament king's chambers without being summoned first. Those who were wise didn't just barge through the doors and say, "Hey, King—wake up, buddy!" And yet our Heavenly Bridegroom says, **"The king has brought me into his chambers."**

As we search or hunger for Him and as we pursue Him and run after Him, what does He do? He brings us into His secret chambers—a place where it's so intimate that no one can go there but His sought-after Bride. Did you know that's why the Lord is drawing us? He's drawing us into that place of intimacy where He can hold and kiss us, changing us into His likeness so that we look just like Him to the world. The same glow that we see on His face makes our own countenance more beautiful. In fact, we actually shine forth the very beauty of the Lord!

Draw me; the king has brought me into his chambers. The Lord is right now calling the church into the chambers of the king, and many in the body of Christ are saying, "Yes, I'm going there!" But some say, "I want to go there but I can't pursue Him because pursuit means consecration, and consecration means crucifying self and giving up some stuff." But we must ask ourselves the question, "Is He worth pursuing? Is His presence worth more than what He is asking of me?" When we sign up at the King's College (the place where we submit ourselves to learn from the Master), some classes aren't easy, but as we submit and consecrate ourselves, He says, "They love Me more than this," and draws us up into the sweet chambers of a king.

At times I haven't felt like praying during my nightly prayer time, but because I knew He was calling me, I prayed anyway. He showed up in an extra special way, rewarding me because I valued my time with Him over the nightly news or a book or a movie that night. And because I gave Him a special gift, a sacrificial gift, He said, "I'm going to show up in a powerful way and change his life." The thing is, God is no respecter of persons, which means this kind of relationship is open to everyone who wants it. That's why I keep writing this kind of message, to stir up hunger inside you!

Again, my prayer at this moment is that, when you finish this book, and you're sitting in your favorite chair, you'll suddenly feel a new, fresh hunger for God that will make you say, "Draw me, Lord." Then you'll begin to run after Him so that He'll welcome you into His chambers which, in turn, will forever change your life.

Draw me, oh Father, that I may run hard after thee. I so long to enter your chambers and stay there. Bid me come fairest, Lord, for I will come and stay, I will dwell in your house forever!

CHAPTER 2

When the Bride Finds Favor with Her Groom

> **"Daughters of kings are among your honored women; at your right hand is the royal bride in gold of Ophir"** (Psalms 45:9).

There's nothing more charming than a woman in love, preparing to wed the man of her dreams, except when that woman is the beloved and beautiful Bride of Christ who is smitten with her King!

In **Psalms 45** we read about an upcoming royal wedding where the queen wears a one-of-a-kind stunning gold gown. The bridegroom, who was also a king, naturally had his pick of all the honorable virgins in the realm. **"Kings' daughters were among thy honorable women..."** But he searched for, and found, his one and only beloved. **"...upon thy right hand did stand the queen in gold of Ophir"** (Psalm 45:9).

At that time, the gold of Ophir was the purest, most valuable gold found anywhere, and this bride wore it from head to toe. As we can only imagine, she was a sight to behold, as she was **"...brought unto the king..."** (v. 14). And because she was completely devoted to her man, with eyes for only him, she was in a class by herself, more beautiful than any other virgin.

Her gown was woven of rare and precious materials, with incredibly fine handwork. Unlike any other gown ever made, its threads were made of pure gold, embellished with dazzling gems.

When her moment came, she walked slowly toward her King with adoring crowds watching, but she only had eyes for Him. Accompanied by an orchestra made up of stringed instruments and horns, the sound was glorious. Following her was a long line of virgins, dressed in white finery, singing and dancing with great rejoicing. Together they approached the waiting groom.

Finally, we see her standing beside her beloved, and the crowd goes wild with joy, because this isn't just any royal wedding. It's the wedding of all time—the royal wedding of our Savior, Jesus Christ and His Bride. **"...the virgins her companions that follow her shall be brought unto thee. With gladness and rejoicing shall they be brought: they shall enter into the king's palace"** (Ps. 45:14-15).

Can you imagine such a sight? The greatest Holy Ghost celebration ever! These nuptials are the culmination—

the very reason for all Creation! The groom, King Jesus, studies His beloved with eyes filled with tender love—toward the redeemed of all mankind, dressed in the very righteousness of Christ! She is gloriously covered in His favor, ready to be His queen!

The Beautifully-Adorned Bride

One morning, as I was waiting on the Lord, I received a vision and saw the throne room. In the center of the room was a woman who knew the wedding was about to begin. She was anxious and glanced around fearfully, asking, "What am I going to wear?" Each time she said this, her face looked increasingly desperate. On her back was written the word "Grace."

Just as her anxiety peaked, a beautiful Bride walked through the door. The "beauty of the Lord" was upon her, as her face was bright, glistening with the light of the glory of God. Her train was very long, shimmering with brilliant rays of light. Her countenance was difficult to gaze at, as the atmosphere of Heaven surrounded her. On her back were written the words, "The righteous acts of the saints."

I continued to pray for some time as the Lord imparted these Scriptures of Revelation 19:7-9 into my heart.

"Let us be glad and rejoice and honor Him. For the time has come for the wedding feast of the Lamb, and His Bride has prepared herself. She

is permitted to wear the finest white linen. (Fine linen represents the good deeds done by those who are overcomers) And the angel said, **'Write this: Blessed are those who are invited to the wedding feast of the Lamb.' And he added, 'These are the true words that come from God'"** (Rev. 19:9, NLT). (Emphasis mine.)

Come up Here

We're living in the end times when the Lord is calling us to walk through an 'open door' into intimacy with Him. The Heavenly Bridegroom is bidding His Bride to "Come up here," (Revelation 4:1) for deeper, more intimate fellowship. And there is but one requirement for admission: hunger—it's open to those who hunger for more of Him. And those who find themselves 'in the spirit' are being progressively changed into His image.

The very glory of God is being poured out upon those who heed this call to "come." In this 'throne room experience', the Bride is being changed from 'glory to glory'. Our Bridegroom desires to pour out the atmosphere of Heaven in our secret places of communion with Him.

As the Church Age transitions into the Kingdom Age, the Body of Christ will be defined by two types of believers; those who only content themselves with the permissive 'grace' of their salvation and, in contrast, the diligent ones—having their eyes fixed on Jesus—who are preparing themselves like the wise virgins of Matthew 25 through their steadfast 'righteous acts', which are not done out of a sense of obligation but rather are birthed out of a love relationship and deep desire to please Him.

The Laodicean Spirit

Today, the 'Laodicean spirit' is running rampant in the Church and has slowly lulled many to sleep. Thus they are not prepared. Our God has called us to "watch at His gate," and to "discern the times." This cunning and pervasive spirit cleverly masks itself, convincing many that they're "rich and increased in goods, and not in need of anything," when instead they are **"wretched, miserable, poor, blind, and naked"** (Rev. 3:15-19).

Today, some churches have replaced the anointed Word of God with rah-rah motivational speeches. They've replaced godly elders with management teams and God-appointed pastors with hired Sunday pulpit ringmasters. They've become more crowd-sensitive than 'spirit-sensitive', relying on their own wisdom rather than divine revelation revealed.

Being 'Spirit-led' has given way to a controlling religious structure that inevitably 'denies the power'. Bereft of God's transforming power it offers only a shallow form of religion, dispensing a creature-developed mindset. They sing songs about the Lord instead of becoming themselves 'a new song'. There is no spontaneous prophetic flow and no move of God.

These have substituted the tickling of the ears—giving misleading information and inadequate, inappropriate encouragement—for true divine revelation. The emphasis is on intellectualism (the rationale of reasoning) rather than purity of heart and mind—'doing' rather than 'being'.

Fool's Gold

In certain areas miners discover a mineral composite called pyrite, a brass-colored substance with a metallic luster. These glittering deposits have lured many a prospector into believing he's struck it rich! Unfortunately, when that 'find' has been duly examined, the essayer will determine that it's worthless! Pyrite is better known by its more familiar name—"fool's gold".

The Devil is an expert counterfeiter and he goes to church! Sadly, such issues also have eternal consequences, for gullible Christians who aren't rooted and grounded in the truth and who often fall prey to a 'lookalike' gospel. It sounds good. It appears authentic, easy to incorporate into their busy lives, and it frequently passes for the real thing. But, like the pyrite, its glitter is only on the surface. The Lord wants us to seek the real thing, with its deeper depths and greater heights.

Laodicean Christian, awake! Let your heart be stirred. Today is the hour of your visitation. Don't be enamored by the falsely religious fool's gold that passes for spiritual nourishment. The risk of being left standing outside the wedding chamber with no oil in your lamp is too great!

As the spirit of Laodicea attempts to blind the eyes of the Body of Christ, Abba Father is busy preparing a beautiful, glorious Bride for His Son. The Bride is 'buying gold tried by fire'—His divine nature. As we allow the fire to burn away our sin we are conformed into the image of His Son. His nature changes our nature and others will say, **"Who is this that comes out of the wilderness, leaning on her lover?"** (Song of Solomon 8:5).

Being the Mature Bride of Christ

The refining fire never feels good. But it's absolutely necessary if we are to be that mature Bride of Christ. In the fire, His Spirit reveals things we must shed so His divine nature can be wrought within us, transforming us from 'glory to glory'. In this process we will embrace His kingdom and fulfill Heavenly mandates. With our invitation in hand, clothed in the garments of His glory, we'll be unashamed by our nakedness on the day of the Marriage Supper of the Lamb. (See Matthew 22:11-14.)

We'll not be frantically searching for something to wear, but rather, through our faithful acts of 'supping with Him', and by answering His 'knocks' on the door of our spirit, we'll be ready and waiting—His stunningly-adorned Bride.

"And they sang a new song, saying, 'You...have made us to our God kings and priests: and we shall reign on the earth'" (Rev. 5:9-10).

Lord, I want to be that mature Bride! I want to be prepared for that special day when we meet at the great Marriage Supper of the Lamb. I refuse to be lukewarm! May my heart never drift toward the things of the world, may it ever burn with passion for you! Lord, light me on fire even now!

CHAPTER 3

The Cry to Go Deeper

"For many are called, but few are chosen"
(Matthew 22:14).

In every generation, there are a few rare individuals who break free from mediocrity and apathy. These trailblazers are hungry for God and yield their lives to follow hard after Him. They yearn for something deeper and more meaningful than a mere surface relationship with the Savior. His beautiful Bride is crying to go deeper into His presence and she is not afraid to run hard after God, living out the deeper life.

We know from Scripture that **"wide is the road that leads to destruction and narrow is the way that leads to life."** (Matt.7:13-14) Hell's highway is very wide with people standing shoulder to shoulder, unknowingly creeping toward the very edge of the abyss. But there is also a narrow road that leads to life, and if you were to sit under a tree beside the road and watch, you would notice that only every so often does anyone pass that way.

Within the body of Christ there's also a broader path called **"status quo."** Many believers are on this road, saved, with Heaven as their final destination, but they fail to seek God's highest or best for their lives. Along this path there's also a narrow gate that leads a few down a path far less traveled. On this path are many twists and turns with bumps and awkward places that require a grand leap of faith to continue on. This is the road called **"sacrifice."** It's a long walk down this rough and lonely road and few want to go that way.

Satisfaction in His Presence

On the road called "status quo," travelers are content with what they've always had. They're enamored by the "blessings" of God. They seek Him for what He can do for them and are content with just the gifts of His hands. They desire a life of ease, comfort, and simplicity. They avoid those who preach about "carrying the cross" or "denying self." It's far easier to seek a popular, "feel good" message.

A rare few travel the path called "sacrifice" and are not content merely to follow the multitudes down a crowded highway. For these saints the only place of deep satisfaction is in His manifest presence, where they can actually touch His face and feel His heartbeat. They're absolutely convinced that the Bridegroom is the only One worth pursuing! They have a kingdom mindset and see things in light of eternity rather than being consumed by the here and now. They cry out with passion, "Draw me Jesus, I want the deeper life found only in You."

So, what does it mean to live the deeper life? It means walking a road far less traveled where consecration, holiness, humility, intimacy, devotion, and sacrifice are treasured—where its travelers would rather invest themselves in pleasing God than in pleasing man. It's a place where the Lord rules and reigns in their hearts and they realize that **crowns aren't simply given away but are earned.** Taking up the cross and following hard after God, though difficult, still brings deep contentment to the soul and is actually its own reward. To them pleasing their Bridegroom means everything!

A life of sacrifice and devotion is a virtue, a sweet fragrance that actually scents the throne room and blesses the heart of God. If we're honest with ourselves, we know that anything less leaves us feeling empty and dissatisfied. It's not good enough to believe that we're devout, just because of the number of prayers we rack up. If we leave church feeling arrogant and angry toward those we say we love, we're only deceiving ourselves. Spiritual maturity must be more than just a desire or an intention—it must be walked out day by day, moment by moment, as we become that pure and holy Bride He desires.

We often fill our lives with useless things and shallow pursuits until we gradually grow weaker and colder until we've finally had enough. At that point a hunger from deep within is born and we rise up and cry out, "I'm desperate for my Heavenly Bridegroom!"

Seeking a Fresh Encounter

Why does it take so long to realize our desperate state and seek the cure? Because it's tough to face the truth we often conceal even from ourselves—that the old way just doesn't cut it anymore. When the Holy Spirit shows us how weak and wayward we are, we then humble ourselves and can only cry out for a fresh encounter with the living God. Nothing else will do. In fact, we feel like we'll die without it. It's only at the place where we will settle for nothing less that we are truly ready to go deep with God.

But be warned. Going hard after God will offend others. It's inevitable—the moment you press into God, Christian friends will show up with "words of encouragement" that are actually motivated by the enemy, designed to quench your fire and stifle the deep hunger inside you. And make no mistake about it, if you act on their words they will lead you back through that narrow gate and onto same old, wide road to nowhere. Better to lose a friend than to miss out on the incredible treasures of being intimate with the Sweet Master.

And while you may offend those close to you by going hard after God, He is pleased and excited by the fervent hunger in your heart. That's why you must silence the conflicting voices around you, whether of humans or spirits or both, that urge you to settle for less than Father's best. To go deep you must predetermine to march to the beat of a different drummer, leaving behind those who refuse to walk the road of sacrifice.

Are you desperate enough to grab God's attention to say that you won't let Him go until you really know Him? Are you tired of standing on the sidelines as a mere spectator while the passionate pass you by? Get desperate enough today to press in. Cry out with all your heart, refusing to settle for anything less than God's best. Get hungry for the deeper things of God, moving beyond the status quo to touch His very heart as His mature Bride.

He Is a Jealous God

In Exodus 34:14 we read this profound statement: **"... for the Lord, whose name is Jealous, is a jealous God"** (Exodus 34:14).

Does that mean we can provoke jealousy in our God? Absolutely. In 1 Corinthians 10:22 we read, **"Do we provoke the Lord to jealousy?"** Here Paul is asking, "You have testified that you love Him. You've even taken His name. Yet, has someone or something else stolen your heart?"

My heart's desire is that we're able to stand before the Bridegroom, so he can say, **"This is My beloved, the very one who spent a great deal of time with Me. You couldn't wait for morning to get up and meet Me, and you always spent time with Me at bedtime. We've had great times together because you were always expectantly waiting to be with Me. We are in harmony, never to be apart again."** His eyes are filled with tender love when He speaks those words. It was His deepest heart's desire.

"Can a maid forget her ornaments, or a bride her attire? yet my people have forgotten me days without number" (Jeremiah 2:32). We dare not let the fire of our love burn low but fan the embers into a flame that changes everything—forever.

In other words, going to church doesn't make you a Bride. A true Bride is one who simply loves Abba more than anyone or anything else and will follow Him wherever He goes. Are you seeking Him with all your heart? That's the question we must answer; our placement in eternity depends on it.

Surrendering to God

Going hard after Father will mean loving Him not just in word but also in deed. Willing surrender is the first step to empowerment and the anointing that comes only when we refuse to settle for anything less than serving

Abba with all our hearts, souls, minds and strength. It's hard to convince our finite minds that carrying a cross can bring peace and contentment, but because it's by His strength that we accomplish anything, He gets the glory and we're filled up in the process.

He is the gentle, exalted Master, and we need only adore Him on this narrow path, even without fully understanding it all, to please Him. By walking the path of sacrifice we finally realize that we can never become mature without first dying to the old, selfish lifestyle that demands more and is never satisfied. In dying to our old man we become that fully developed "new man" that God intended—something that could never happen otherwise. (See Eph. 4:22-24)

As we walk down the narrow path of sacrifice He accomplishes His grand design for our lives. We become reliant on Him and He frees us from self by revealing our weaknesses by the power of the Holy Spirit. An intense desperation is created by the emptiness we find in all earthly things, which hold little appeal at that point. We discover the doorway to the deeper life by first being discontent with a shallow, egocentric existence.

The natural man would love to go deep in Christ and His pure love at no cost, but it's only his excessive self-love and pride that acts so childish and demanding in the first place. And while the fatherly heart of God takes no joy in seeing us struggle, He knows the road of sacrifice brings about steadfastness and meekness, purifying our motives and intentions to the point where we are worthy to feel His deepest heart cries and carry His message of love to a lost and dying world.

Take heart, precious friend, when bearing the cross down the narrow and winding road of sacrifice as you anticipate the joy that comes with pressing in. As you go hard after Father, let me encourage you. You have set out on a journey of divine proportions, determined to settle for nothing less than touching the very heart of Abba, and I guarantee that in that place is fullness of joy, where you will find that the Bridegroom is altogether lovely and everything you ever wanted!

Deeper, Lord, deeper is where I long to be! I will not stop at your outer court, I will not just observe others dwelling with you in the secret place, but I will lay down in your glory and rest in your manifest presence! I am after your heart!

CHAPTER 4

A Holy Desperation

"By night on my bed I sought him whom my soul loveth: I sought him, but I found him not" (Song of Solomon 3:1).

The *Shulamite* girl of the Song of Solomon found herself in a season of darkness, pursuing her Lover but unable to find Him. A deep yearning caused her to rise up and pursue the object of her affection.

"<u>And I said I will rise now</u>, and go about the city in the streets, and in the broad ways <u>I will seek him</u> whom my soul loveth: I sought him, <u>but I found him not</u>" (v.2).

As darkness began to fall, she grew increasingly desperate to find her one true love, but her search was in vain.

Alone and anxious, she felt abandoned and afraid, unable to sense His presence anywhere. I can see her face—her eyes dark and haunted, feeling terribly lost and confused. She walked all alone with no one to comfort her until she reached out to a watchman and cried out in desperation, **"Have you seen the one my heart loves?"** (v.3) With no response, she turned away. Disappointed, she walked on alone.

All at once, in the darkness of the night she discovered Him!

"Scarcely had I passed them when I found the one my heart loves. I held him and would not let him go" (v.4).

She embraced Him and refused to let go! The yearning and desire did deep work inside her. She could now rest, reunited with the one who was **"altogether lovely."** (Song of Solomon 5:16) Through a dark night she discovered a deep longing that could only be satisfied by finding Him.

At some point, you as a maturing Bride will face a dark night when it seems that all is lost, so that your spiritual vision has become blurred—when you can't sense the nearness of His presence or reach out and touch Him. You will feel like asking, "Where has He gone?" The sense of abandonment is palpable, and Abba feels a million miles away. Perhaps you're in that battle now.

You reach out to others, but they don't understand, nor can they help you. All at once, you discover inside a deep desperation that you didn't know existed. It propels you from that place of spiritual apathy into a full-blown pursuit of your Bridegroom. Your spiritual hunger begins to grow within you by leaps and bounds.

It might help to know that there's a purpose to the dark night of the soul—because we feel alone, anxious and desperately needy, we're especially motivated to earnestly seek our one true love. If we understood what was going on, we would actually short-circuit the process. It's the not knowing that creates a yearning for God, motivating us to rise up to pursue Him. We must permit it to run its course to accomplish God's objectives in our lives.

Darkness always vanishes with the sunrise. And with it comes hope; you're facing a brand-new season. With this new day comes the revelation that you were never alone, even in the darkness of the night. His presence was still there with you, yet it was hidden so that you would desire Him and pursue Him above all else. Do you love Him most?

Before apathy falls away we experience heartache and pain in our desperate search. Self is set aside when we realize our desire for God can be satisfied only by God Himself. Everything else fades in importance compared to being in His presence during the dark night of the soul.

If you're in a dark season, it's time to rise up, Bride of Christ, and pursue the object of your affection! Wait on the Lord and refuse to go by your feelings; just know that morning is coming when you will soar high on wings like eagles. You will run and not grow weary. You will walk and not faint! (Is. 40:31)

The phrase "dark night of the soul" sounds like a threatening and much-to-be-avoided experience. If we in no way experienced the chill of a dark and cold winter, it is very unlikely that we would ever cherish the warmth of a brilliant summer's day. In the dark night we learn to beseech God, with great yearnings, as He takes from us our imperfections and faults. **It's in the dark night that we receive a holy desperation for our Heavenly Bridegroom.**

If I Can Just Touch Him!

"Who touched me?" Jesus asked. When they all denied it, Peter said, "Master, the people are crowding and pressing against you." But Jesus said, "Someone touched me; I know that power has gone out from me" (Luke 8:45-46).

Consider this question: Have you been feeding on the garbage of the world for so long that you've lost your desperation for your Heavenly Bridegroom? Many who are believed to belong to Him live day to day without an ounce of passion for Him, with little more than an empty, distorted intellectual grasp and no connection to His heart. But it's time for that to change. The Bridegroom is calling you to a place of holy desperation before Him, for He longs to hear you cry out to Him with all your heart. He longs to see you lay prostrate before Him with your arms open wide, asking Him to touch you once more.

It has always been Satan's ploy to keep you so full of the junk of this world that you're no longer desperate for Him and His presence. Don't give into his distractions; don't let him pull you into apathy, but let your Bridegroom woo you back to your first love and stir up the dying embers inside you that long for more of Him!

Many within the church only go through the motions, praying halfhearted prayers, which is why they see no answers. The King wants you to fall in love with Him again, to cry out with a fresh desperation for Him. He will not turn away a heart that's on fire with love for Him.

Consider the woman with the issue of blood. Her desperation tapped into His power with a breakthrough faith that compelled her to elbow her way through the crowd to get to Him. She was pale and weak, having suffered twelve years with uterine bleeding. Doctors could not help her; instead of getting better, she grew worse.

She knew Jesus was her only hope. Even in her weakened state she refused to give up hope that He could heal her. So desperate was her need that she continued to pursue Him until she finally reached the place where He stood.

She had decided in her heart, **"If I can just touch His clothes, I'll be healed"** (Mark 5:28). Until that moment she'd been hopeless, but a tiny seed of hope had begun to bloom inside her. Her illness had made her an outcast, unclean and untouchable, yet, in the end, her faith made her whole. And He is still a God of restoration today!

Even as she touched the edge of His cloak and He instantly felt the tug of her faith, He will take notice when you reach out and pull against His heart! She was instantly healed by the virtue that flowed from within Him, and you too will be healed as you dare to reach out and touch your Bridegroom with desperate faith.

Would your faith be enough to constrain Him? By that I mean would your case 'compel, urge or press with urgency'? Do you consider Him so precious and rare that you refuse to leave His side, no longer satisfied with a casual encounter or an intellectual grasp of who He is? Your desperate faith is what draws Him close in a way nothing else can. So, will you reach out to Him and refuse to take no for an answer?

He will not walk past a heart that desperately constrains Him to come. He will make His habitation with you when you truly pursue Him with all your heart in faith. Cry out with all your heart, mind and strength; call out His name and He will come and minister to the needs of your heart.

Even as He said in Jeremiah 29:12-13, **"In those days when you pray, I will listen. If you look for me <u>wholeheartedly</u>, you will find me."**

Sometimes He'll allow circumstances to stir up a desperate search for Him, so that He can display His power to fulfill your greatest need—for Him.

The truth is that none of these things will make sense to you until you search for Him as you would search for silver, until you seek for Him as you would seek hidden treasure. (Prov. 2:4) Only then will you find everything you need in Him, for He is the only true riches, and in Him you will find hope, healing, restoration, revelation—and ultimately peace.

His overcoming Bride has an unfathomable desperation that burns from within. She will not be satisfied until she has the one her soul loves most, the very lover of her soul—Jesus!

I will not fall prey to apathy or a lukewarm spirit; I am desperate for you, my Heavenly Bridegroom. I hear your feet coming toward me now. I am open for you, oh Abba. I push through any darkness and pursue you with all my heart! You are my hidden treasure!

CHAPTER 5

The Bride Who Presses In

It was on a Thursday night in the year 2006 after my wife and I had started a small group that sought to welcome the presence of the Lord in western Michigan. We had rented an inexpensive hotel meeting room where a handful of people were gathered that night to seek the Lord. We set a chair on the front altar by the pulpit. It was a special chair we dedicated as a symbolic gesture to say, "Jesus, we want you to come and rest in this place—be our honored guest!"

I'd just finished speaking about "creating a resting place of His presence." We were praying, pressing into God, asking for a deeper hunger for more of Him. My wife looked up and saw Jesus walk physically into the room and sit down on the appointed chair set out for Him. He looked beautiful and comfortable as He smiled as if to say, "I've found a special place I can come and rest." All at once, He was gone.

Later, someone else mentioned that they too had seen the Lord physically walk into the room. As hard as it is to believe, my wife and I stand in absolute integrity before the Lord when we testify of these events. I believe our pressing and hunger as well the creating of a special place for Him to rest compelled the Lord to come and rest with us. **The Heavenly Bridegroom will have a Bride that knows how to press in.**

In fact, for some time now the Lord has been speaking to me about the word "pressing". What does it mean to press? I used the word "constraining" earlier so what does it mean to "constrain the Lord"? When you hear the word "constrain," sometimes you think in terms of restraining or limiting someone's activity. But, when I use the word "constrain," I'm talking about a tugging or pulling on someone.

To constrain, to pull or press speaks of a heart attitude that desperately seeks to be near the Bridegroom. Someone who's eager and excited to be His lover and friend. I long to see a generation with a holy hunger press into God. They have a desire to constrain the Lord, to come and abide with Him.

In Strong's Concordance, "constrain" is defined as to compel, to urge and to press. This is not an ordinary request; it's a persistent, heart-felt yearning and the result is pressing in and staying close, listening, able to hear the still, small voice of the Spirit. It's a heart that pushes for a deeper level of fellowship that's not satisfied with a casual encounter.

How many people do we know right now who want nothing more than casual encounter with God? "Oh God, just come and bless me." "Oh God, just do something." But they're not compelling Him to come and to stay close. I find that if we compel Him—if we're really hungry for Him, if we press in—He'll come and meet with us and take us far deeper.

But we face a dilemma—we love our watches. And if the Lord doesn't come after five minutes, we give up and grow weary of waiting then go on to the next activity. If we don't see results after an hour, we become discouraged. We need to ask the question, "Is the yearning so deep in me that I can't help but call out to Him, 'Jesus, son of David, come into my life and move by your Spirit. Come by your Spirit and talk to me! Come by your Spirit and walk through my home. I want you 24/7. Jesus, my Heavenly Bridegroom come turn my life upside down!'"

Is it just a prayer—something you say without conviction—or do you mean it with all your heart and all your guts? Because, if it means everything to you and you refuse to give up in defeat, He'll come and move in your life, but He wants to know you mean business. Do you really mean business? Many say they want to press in, but when tested they fail to stay the course until He comes.

No Matter How Long It Takes....

I shared a story from my life from the year of 1993 in my book, *Whispers from the Throne Room*. I felt the Lord wanted me to share this story with you again.

"And the LORD said unto Moses, I will do this thing also that thou hast spoken: for thou hast found grace in my sight, and I know thee by name" (Ex. 33:17).

When I first began in the ministry, I was so hungry to see Father move in my life that I truly wanted to hear His voice. Since I was born in a pastor's home, it was not unusual to see my parents have major encounters with the Lord. My father could literally hear the voice of God speaking to him. It also seemed as if my mother had a direct line to the Lord. Whenever I did something wrong, Abba would always tell her. It seemed like I couldn't get away with anything; my mother always knew because the Lord would tell her.

I wanted that same kind of relationship my parents had with the Lord as they lived the Word in front of me. They didn't just preach one thing from a pulpit and live another way at home. On Saturday nights I would drive by the church and my dad's light would be on in his office, where he was seeking the Lord. The next Sunday it seemed as if the Holy Spirit had given him notes on what to say during his message because it hit so many different people in such a personal way. They were blessed because my dad seemed to be speaking about what they were going through when they hadn't even told him about it.

I accepted without question the fact that the Lord spoke to my dad. He also spoke to my mom, a great woman of prayer and intercession. Whenever I think of her, I picture her kneeling beside her bed, praying for hours at a time. In fact, I remember walking into her room one day, picking up her Bible, which was completely worn out, and seeing the tear stains that had dried on its pages. I knew that if Abba could speak to my parents in that way, there was no reason why He couldn't speak to me as well.

"I will climb up to my watchtower and stand at my guard post. There I will wait to see what the Lord says..." (Habakkuk 2:1).

I went to prayer a desperate man, fully aware that it was possible to hear Father's voice. I had not been raised to separate the spiritual from the physical realms. The Lord was very real to me, not just a fairy tale or some grown-up version of Let's Pretend. I prayed for about an hour and yet nothing happened; I didn't feel a single goose bump. I didn't feel anything at all. It was as if the heavens were brass and God was ignoring me. I prayed for another hour, and still nothing happened.

I prayed constantly for three hours and still nothing happened. After about three and a half hours, I couldn't help thinking I should just give up—God wasn't going to speak to me. But something deep inside me compelled me to stay in His presence. I knew I had to keep going, I had to have the same tenacity as Jacob when he wrestled with that angel.

The Lord's presence entered the room and I began to weep uncontrollably. The wind of the Spirit literally blew through the church! When He spoke, it wasn't an audible voice, but it might as well have been because it was so loud in my spirit that there was no question that it was His voice and not something I dreamed up. I will never forget what He said:

"Steve, I am the God of Abraham, Isaac, and Jacob, and I am the God of Steve Porter too."

I wept for over an hour after that as I lingered in His presence because God actually knew my name. I was special to Him. Nobody outside of my small community may have known my name, but the Creator of heaven and Earth did. After all the pain of humiliation and rejection I had endured from my enemies all those years, Abba knew me by name... My friend, He knows your name too!

Jesus the sweet Bridegroom is truly worth pursuing no matter what it takes. If you have to pursue and pray and fast for weeks or hours a day, then do it. Just do it. Press in and constrain the Lord to come and manifest Himself to you, resisting the temptation to give up before you see it happen. If you want more of Abba, don't take no for an answer because He wants that kind of fellowship with you more than you could even dream. Don't give up. Never give up! Pursue Him as if your life depended on it because, in these end times, it really does!

Walter Beuttler- "A Man Who Knew How to Press into God"

"¹² Then you will call on me and come and pray to me, and I will listen to you. ¹³ You will seek me and find me when you seek me with all your heart" (Jeremiah 29:12-13).

At this point, I want to remember a very special man by the name of Walter Buettler, who had a powerful influence on my life. Walter was born in Germany in 1904. He immigrated to the U.S. in 1925. In 1931, he graduated from the Central Bible Institute. He served on the faculty at the Eastern Bible Institute from 1939 to 1972. During a campus revival in 1951, God called Beuttler to "go teach all nations," and for twenty-two years he traveled the world ministering the Word of God. At that point, he retired in Shaverton, PA with his wife Elizabeth. There he continued to minister until he went to be with the Lord at the age of seventy.

The Lord often visited the classroom as he taught and revealed Himself, clearly moving in the lives of the students who sat under Walter's ministry. At the end of each visitation, brother Beuttler would smile at his students and say, "Isn't He nice?" He often exhorted his students to cultivate that kind of personal, experiential knowledge of the Lord.

Walter used his unique spiritual walk and experiences with the Lord as a means to encourage others to begin seeking the Lord in earnest. Brother Beuttler went beyond seeking God for His blessings to seek God for Himself. He traveled the world many times over teaching about his friend—Jesus. The presence of God was electrifying in his meetings because he personally knew and walked with the Lord as very few others I know.

One student who sat under his ministry explained in his own words: *"We often experienced firsthand exactly what he was teaching us when the Holy Spirit would suddenly fall over the classroom with his wondrous sense of presence. 'Students, close your books, he is here.' Quietly we would close our books and slip our notes inside our Bibles. Then we would start waiting and breathing in the presence of the Holy Spirit. A message in another language would be heard and a word of interpretation would follow giving the class direction or admonishing us. The rest of the class period was given to praying and several others could be heard weeping as the Holy Spirit was doing His work secretly in the heart of each student."* — *Bill Burkett*

Walter Beuttler's ministry has deeply affected my life in ways I find it hard to express. He passed away in 1974, yet his ministry still lives on through his sermons and articles. I have spent hours reading and studying

Draw Me

his life, and each time I receive a greater hunger for the manifest presence of God.

Brother Beuttler once told the story of how he'd been watching another pastor's church for a week, and the Lord told him to fast and pray, saying, "Don't eat anything." So that night he went into the church and began to seek the Lord in earnest. He prayed all night and into the next day and still nothing happened. That night he went to sleep, still fasting, and when he woke, he returned to the church and continued to pray. But halfway through his fast, he grew despondent because the Spirit of God wasn't moving, so he decided to give up the fast.

Now, I know you don't know Walter Beuttler, so you have no reason to trust him, but I trust this man and his word because I have listened to all his sermons and read all his writings, and I know he's a credible source whose stories are true. I have interviewed many people who knew him personally and they all testify to his integrity. That day, he went home and sat down to eat. As soon as he put the first spoonful of food in his mouth, the Devil appeared in front of him and began to laugh. As a result, he instantly dropped the spoon and returned to the church. He resumed praying and began to contend, by then simply waiting on the Lord for direction. He continued his fast for the rest of the week, fasting for seven days. By then his heart was desperately hungry for the Lord to move in his midst. But it seemed the Lord was taking an awfully long time. At that point he encouraged himself, saying, "He's worth pursuing."

It was the last night of his fast, when he was alone at the altar, that he felt chilly, so he covered himself with newspapers and continued to lie on his face on the floor, saturating himself in the presence of God. In that instant, he literally saw Jesus enter the room. Jesus spoke to Walter, telling him things that He would not reveal to anyone else because they were too special and personal. But the deep personal revelation he received profoundly changed him and his ministry from that day on.

His example is a great testimony to me. Most of us would give up the fast, the pressing in, by the third day, believing Jesus would've spoken by that time if He intended to. However, I believe the truth is far different than we imagine. Our Heavenly Bridegroom is quite anxious to speak to us, but the question is how badly do we want to hear what He has to say? Do you really want Him to come and change your life? Only you can decide what it's worth to press in for everything Abba has for you. Only you can fast and pray for breakthroughs and direction, for the deep things that are only acquired by pressing in.

The Heavenly Bridegroom will have a Bride who knows what it means to press in—who knows what it means to contend—who knows what it means to constrain the Lord, refusing to take "no" for an answer. Have you ever heard someone say, "We'll have to have you over for dinner sometime soon"? If so, you probably didn't take the invitation seriously, because it was too vague, and you probably wondered if the invitation was serious. But if that person said, "I want you to come to dinner—how about Thursday night at six?" you'd know it was a serious invitation, and you'd probably rearrange your schedule to accommodate it because the host meant business. They pulled on you to come.

The Lord is much like that potential guest. He wants to know we're serious about spending time pressing in to seek and pursue His face. If we're flippant when we say, "I want more of you, God," He's well aware of the lack of sincerity behind it. On the other hand, He's eager to respond to those who cry from a deep heart need, **"Come, Jesus. I'm desperate for more of you. I can't live without you, so I'm pressing in, expecting you to give me more."**

This message is vital for those who want to be lovers of God in these end times. In fact, I hope this message wakes you in the night—that you can't get it out of your mind. That it makes you hungry and thirsty for more of Abba, unwilling to settle for less, because they're the people in whom Father invests His time, to whom He reveals His deep secrets and perfumes with His presence. Don't settle for less than His best! The beautiful face of your Bridegroom is looking your way—His outstretched arms tenderly desire to pull you ever so close. Press in!

I desire to be a lover of Abba alone. Nothing can compare with you! You alone satisfy the inner longings of my heart! I will not settle for anything but you! I must have you, I must!

CHAPTER 6

The King's College

"You Shall have a song as in the night when a holy feast is kept, and gladness of heart..."
(Isa. 30:29a).

If you've heard me speak or you've read my writings, you'll know I talk and write a lot about **the Lord's visits in the night.** And for me to completely cover the subject of the Bride I need to touch on it again. It's very close to my heart.

Who are we that our Heavenly Bridegroom would invite us to spend time with Him during the night hours? When others are tucked away in bed, it's an amazing thing to keep company with the Lord. Some of my most unforgettable times have been the nights when I enjoyed a holy feast. The truth is that a holy feast is available to all who will sacrifice their comfort and get up to meet with their God.

There is a school that meets at night. **It's the *King's College*.** This school takes no money but requires obedience far beyond what is usually required. Not many will pay the price. Attending this school may cost them more than they can handle.

Feasting at the Lord's table at night is more rewarding than I can explain in mere words. The truth is that some things are better caught then taught. When you grasp the treasure of feasting on His presence and sitting at His table, you will never be the same again.

I'm amazed that I would even be allowed to keep the Lord *company* at night—that I could ever touch His heart. Yet, His heart is moved when I attend the *King's College* and sit at His feet to hear His heart, to love on Him or just be silent relishing the moment of such Holy Communion.

"My beloved is like a roe or a young hart: behold, he standeth behind our wall, he looketh forth at the windows, shewing himself through the lattice" (Song of Solomon 2:9).

Rise Up, My Darling!

The Heavenly Bridegroom stands outside the wall looking through the window. He waits patiently for us and calls out softly, *"Rise up, My darling! Come away with me, my fair one!"* Then He waits for our response. Will we agree to "come away"? Will we leave our warm beds and the distractions of the world and come away? Will we leave our normal routine and sit with Him awhile?

He shows Himself, letting us know He is there. He looks through the window, slowly revealing His presence, and hopes we will notice Him. Do we? Or do we sit alone, content with the blessings He has provided, while the Lord of glory is alone and lonely? And, as hard as it is to believe, He longs for our company, for intimacy with us. He wants us to know we have a higher purpose. He yearns for us to go deeper and bask in His presence, in His arms, where we can finally rest and find true contentment and security.

Our Heavenly Bridegroom is not content that we merely hear stories about His manifest presence. He wants us to draw near and enjoy fellowship with Him in the secret place. He longs to bring us into the experiential reality of His manifest presence. It's there that He awakens the desire for more of Him and reveals the deeper things of the Spirit.

The word 'manifest' means to make visible to one or more of our five senses. Within that sacred precinct are the very chambers where we enter His manifest presence. Because the Lord has been repeatedly wounded by those who take His presence carelessly, He is hesitant to openly make known Himself to them. Therefore, He cautiously approaches those He seeks (looking through the window) to discover whether we really desire Him or if it's mere lip service.

Do we relate only to His 'omnipresence', which includes merely a sense of divine presence but stops there without going further? The omnipresence is just a doorway leading us into His manifest presence where we meet Him as a person and have a personal visitation from a personal Christ.

His Head Wet with Dew

"Open to me, my darling, my treasure, my lovely dove, he said, for I have been out in the night. My head is soaked with dew, my hair with the wetness of the night" (SOS 5:2b, NLT).

His head can become wet with the dew of the night when we don't get up to let Him get out of the night air and into our homes. This is a beautiful prophetic picture of our Heavenly Bridegroom coming to us for intimacy. He announces His coming with His presence. He knocks on our door at night, longing to be with us. His head is soaked with the dampness of the cool night air. Why is His hair wet? Perhaps, ours is not the first house He visited that night. He knocks at each door, longing to enter for intimate communion but is instead met with rejection and excuses. As he wipes the tears away, He moves on to the next house hoping for obedience, all the while gathering more dew on His head.

He is longing to enter our homes; He wants to find a quiet place to rest. He desires someone to keep Him company in the night. Will you be that person? Can He count on you to meet Him anytime He calls? It's easy to meet with Him in the day, but only His choicest servants meet with Him in the night. The sacrifice is a small price to pay for His companionship. How much value do we place on our meetings with Him? Do we desire His company more than the air we breathe? When we value Him more than costly treasures, His presence will be ours to enjoy.

Walter Beuttler

As I said, Walter Beuttler was a powerful example to me—he knew how to keep the Lord company in the night. When I'm extremely tired and tempted to go back to sleep, the testimony of Brother Beuttler compels me to awaken and sit before the Lord. He has left a lantern for us to follow. The following is a story in Walter's own words that has stuck with me throughout the years. I hope it's as special and memorable to you too.

"Down at school around 1950, the Lord had given me a tremendous hunger to seek Him. I had that many years before, but didn't follow through, but then it came back. I sought the Lord in between all my schoolwork. Schoolwork is heavy, and I'm out in ministry all the time. Every weekend I'm somewhere. Still, I sought the Lord in every crack of time I had, especially by night. I get up during the night, many times in the middle of the night for no other reason than to seek Him, to worship Him, to sit in His presence (*unfelt* presence), simply sit there. That went on for some time, then the Lord began to reveal Himself.

"One night, He walked into our cottage. I heard Him step by step as He moved through the cottage; heard Him turn around and then speak to me in an audible voice. On one of those nights, I was sitting there simply admiring Him. I got up about 2:30 admiring Him, keeping Him company. I said, '*Lord, so many of Your people are asleep now, and I want to get up to spend a little time with You to keep You company.*'

"I had the clearest perception of the Lord walking toward me from behind. I didn't see Him, but had the perception of it. It was as real as could be. I perceived Him bending over me from behind, and literally felt a sensation of drops falling on top of my head. I instinctively knew this sensation was the teardrops of His appreciation for somebody who would get up in the middle of the night for no other reason than to keep Him company. Now that happened only once, receiving tokens of His appreciation. The Lord loves to do that."

Here is another story of Walter Beuttler in his own words:

"Now God hears what I say. I had sought the Lord for hours upon hours during the night, deprived myself of sleep. *I wanted Him*. I sought no experience, simply Him, out of a great hunger, when one night I was awakened by a man singing, a man's voice singing in my bedroom. It woke me up; the voice awakened me, and there stood the Lord by the window, full size, in white garments, looking my way, singing two stanzas for me of a song that I've never heard before or since. And then He was gone.

"'He that hath my commandments, and keepeth them, he it is that loveth me: and he that loveth me shall be loved of my Father, and I will love him, <u>and will manifest myself to him</u>' (John 14:21).

"Other translations read:

"'I will manifest myself to him; I will disclose myself to him; I will show myself to him, I will plainly show myself to him.'

"If you take the Pulpit Commentary, and check on this verse, it says that this word '*manifest*' in the Greek is so strong as to mean *nothing less than a manifestation of the Lord perceivable by our physical senses.* You can check on this yourself. I've had the experience, so I'm very much assured of it. *Here the Lord will <u>give us tokens of appreciation for our appreciation of Him</u>* [1]."

—Walter Beuttler

The teardrops of the Lord falling on Brother Beuttler's head... Can you imagine? What an honor that we could touch the heart of God! Also he shared, "as we appreciate Him He will appreciate us!" Our Heavenly Bridegroom is inviting His Bride to spend time with Him! May we get up and enter the King's College—The Bridal Training School and keep Him company even in the night! We'll talk more about this subject as we continue on this journey together. I feel led to take a moment right now to seek the Lord with you.

I see you standing alone looking through the window. I won't keep you standing there. I will bid you come and sit with me in sweet intimacy. Reveal yourself to me, for I'm not content with just hearing stories of your presence. I want to discover you myself! Lord, I want to keep you company in the night while others are tucked away in bed. I want to sit up with you and just love on you. I embrace you, I treasure you, and I want to have a holy feast unto you. I want to be a constant companion of my Father! Lord, I refuse to allow your head to be covered with dew from the night. I will meet you in our secret place. I will answer you when you call. When you announce your presence, I will open the door to my heart. Come in, dearest Lord, and commune with me! I bid you come!

1. Laws Governing the Presence - Walter Beuttler

CHAPTER 7

One Glance from His Eyes

"You have stolen my heart, my sister, my bride; you have stolen my heart with one glance of your eyes, with one jewel of your necklace"
(Song of Solomon 4:9).

Why do I believe what I believe? It can be summed up in one word—"relationship". It's not about slavishly following a long list of authoritarian rules lest I anger God. It's all about knowing Him personally and wanting to please Him. The religious leaders in Jesus' day firmly claimed to know God but killed Jesus when He came to rescue mankind. Jesus unsympathetically rebuked them for their hard hearts and blatant, unrepentant hypocrisy. When we know Jesus in a personal way, we can't help but love and desire Him. In turn, we will try to obey Him because we know He has our very best interests in mind.

My dad has also been a real inspiration to me. He has great integrity, and I've never in all my years heard him tell a lie. He's always been honest with me even when it hurt. I've admired his deep desire to really know Jesus as a friend, not merely as a legendary historical figure. It stems from a time when he was fifteen years old. Let me explain.

Dad lived on the ocean in Maine. His family came from a long line of Canadian commercial fishermen. My grandmother was a deeply dedicated Christian lady who ministered with my grandpa. She was a pastor, a Bible school professor, and an inner city relief worker reaching out to the destitute and needy—the "down and out". It was said of my grandmother that she never said an unkind word about anyone. I loved her so much.

One night, at age fifteen, my dad went to bed, pondering what he should do with his life. He was wide awake and not sleeping when Jesus walked into the room and stood at the foot of his bed. He opened His hands to my dad so that the nail prints were clearly visible. My dad said he had never seen such great love before. The eyes of Jesus moved Him to tears.

At that moment Dad was transformed forever. He cried all night after that because Jesus loved him so much. The eyes of Jesus told the true story; no one would be able to tell Him otherwise. He'd had a personal visitation from a personal Savior. Just as the early disciples dropped what they were doing to follow Jesus by reason of "one gaze from His eyes," after one look my dad knew what he was called to do. Most people don't have such awe-inspiring encounters with their physical eyes. My dad was incredibly blessed by that life-changing incident and it became very apparent in his ministry.

Turn your head, precious one; He's looking your way with eyes full of love. One look will transform your life. His head is turned toward you, His beautiful Bride, right now! When you look at Him, you steal His heart. Can you see Him? With His arms open wide, He desires to embrace you and tenderly lead you away into His presence. Take the hand of the Master, for He is waiting for you in the secret place!

In fact, did you know that both His eyes and thoughts have been on you since the day you were conceived? You may be surprised to learn that scripture says you're always on His mind. [17] **How precious are your thoughts about me, O God. They cannot be numbered!** [18] **I can't even count them; they outnumber the grains of sand. And when I wake up, you are still with me!** (Psalms 139:17-18)

Divinely Inspired

"Divinely Inspired."

Those two words are often thrown around when people reflect on the arts and other achievements that are truly remarkable—human works that deeply move us.

But what does that phrase really mean?

Think about this for a moment: when a man puts brush to canvas and produces art that moves those who gaze on it, is that irrefutable proof that God's hand moved through that artist? Of course not.

The only people who can make that claim are the artists themselves. And God, of course. But every now and then we find a piece of art that is so provocative that those two words—divinely inspired—leap into our minds.

Hold that thought for a moment if you will.

Let's walk back in time to when Jesus Christ roamed the Holy Land.

We all *know* that He is divine; after all, He's the Son of God!

But let's take ourselves back to that time, imagining what it was like to actually see the Son of God strolling around, teaching, talking, praying and essentially living a life that was both ordinary for those times and yet extraordinary because of the awesome works He performed.

Imagine being Zacchaeus (Luke 19:2), who was so impassioned by the words he'd been hearing from the Christ that he just had to have Jesus spend time with him in his home, breaking bread together.

So he ran ahead of the crowds following Jesus, guessing where He would be speaking and holding forth, when he spied a tree nearby and scaled it to wait for Jesus.

Luke 19:5 – **"When Jesus looked up…"**

This Man, this Teacher, with two ordinary human eyes—possibly brown in color just like most others in the region—*looked up…*

Think of the sheer power in that gaze. Looking up into a tree where a grown man perched, and telling that guy to "Hurry down! I want to stay with you today."

Boom!

This was the very same gaze that chased a horde of demons into a herd of pigs.

This was the very gaze that touched Lazarus and raised him from the dead.

This was the very same gaze that reduced a crowd of angry men, ready to stone a woman, into a gang of sniveling cowards who guiltily crept away into the shadows, transforming the woman's entire life and the lives of those around her.

Okay, now that you have that image fixed firmly in your mind—think about the way the loving gaze of Christ could and often did change their very lives, shaking them to their very core, trampling underfoot the false doctrine that salvation depended on following the Law of Moses.

Now, imagine Christ turning that stunning gaze…

On you.

Back to the thought on the phrase "divinely inspired".

There is such a work in which that phrase can be ascribed. <u>There is a painting of Jesus Christ</u>, created roughly fifteen hundred years ago, where He is holding a Bible and making a sign of blessing. It's on display in St. Catherine's monastery in the Sinai Desert somewhere.

Take a look at it if you will. Follow this safe link: **www.pohick.org/Images/pantocrator.jpg**

Look at His eyes in that painting. Do they look ... unusual?

I was struck by His eyes in that painting. The left eye looks angry. The right looks ... compassionate?

Why would the artist paint the Christ's gaze that way?

Don't be distracted by what His hands are doing. Let's focus on His eyes in this painting.

The left eye is definitely different in appearance. Note the arched eyebrow as compared to the brow of the right eye. Note the *nature* of that left eye in the painting. What does it *provoke*? Anger? Conviction? Unrest?

Now study His right eye. It appears to reflect the opposite emotion of the left. I sense zero anger in that right eye.

Draw Me

Now, there's speculation that the dichotomy in His gaze in this work depicts the duality of ultimate emotion; one being unyielding and unflinching rage, and the other being the single greatest depiction of love that's ever been captured in a piece of art.

Let's not consider what that dichotomy actually represents at this time; no, for now, let's consider the sheer power of that gaze. When we study that painting—I mean really allow ourselves to become immersed in it—it moves us powerfully. It drives us to serious introspection. In short...

It provokes us.

Let's revisit the moment when Jesus turned that powerful, convicting left eye and that deep, boundlessly loving right eye on a simple guy like Zacchaeus.

Or imagine the Christ, amid a crowd of people who were listening to Him teach, suddenly being rudely interrupted by an angry mob of guys who throw an unfortunate woman in front of Him and start pelting Him with questions in a lame attempt to trap Him.

Now imagine that crowd going silent at this sudden confrontation—and then the Christ rises to His feet and turns that gut-wrenching gaze on the Pharisee that's peppering Him with thinly-guised questions designed to expose Jesus for the fraud the Pharisees believed Him to be. Imagine that left eye boring a hole into that Pharisee...

While the right eye evokes sorrow for that very same Pharisee.

All this before the Christ does anything else.

Do you think that Pharisee was quaking in his sandals?

And then, in that very same story, Jesus turns that gaze on the poor woman accused of being an adulteress. He looks at her directly, squarely, turning the sheer power of that gaze on her before He says two simple things that absolutely rock her to her very core.

"...Neither shall I condemn you." Right eye!

"Now go and sin no more." Left eye!

With this in mind, take a look at that painting. Look closely; look deeply; study His gaze and let it sink in; let it provoke your thoughts and let the simple truths inherent here grow increasingly clear to you...

That God *despises* sin!

That God *loves* us with an unfathomable intensity!

Now *that* is divine inspiration! If we are to be the mature bride of Jesus we must understand both eyes and desire to reflect the very glory of God in all we do and say, with nothing lacking. If we can keep the lesson of His eyes before us, knowing that He loves us more than life itself, yet He despises sin, we will want to lose ourselves in His presence and decrease so others may see Him in us.

Isn't It Time to Be Transformed?

Why do you hesitate to turn to Him?

What's in the way? Shame over the sins you've committed? You know what they are; they weigh you down beneath a heavy load of guilt. You can't escape the misery and shame you feel, wondering how He could ever accept you after what you've done.

He already knows your history; and it changes nothing. His love for you is as all-consuming as it has been since before you were born.

Raise your eyes and look at Him; don't be afraid. Refuse to feel shame—just hand it all to Him because, once you've repented of it, He remembers it no more, ever.

Isn't it time to be transformed?

It's really such a simple thing to bare one's soul before the Lord. It means letting go, freeing yourself of the shackles of pride and shame and putting yourself in His Hands totally and completely. It's in this place you'll find His tender mercies that never fail.

Faith is most easily found in the valleys rather than the peaks of your life. But you must allow yourself to find that valley that forces you to cry out and beg forgiveness—to be washed from the inside out; to feel the fire of redemption roar through your soul, scorching your sins into oblivion.

So, is it shame that hinders your willingness to turn to Christ? Or perhaps you haven't found that valley yet; despair hasn't clamped a death-grip around your heart, causing you to cry out in deep desperation.

Despair is the tool of the enemy—that which the enemy believes will cause you to turn away from Jesus.

But the joke is on Him because when we're at our very worst, having hit rock bottom, reaching and clawing just to take a cleansing breath, to get a moment's relief from the crushing weight of despair—that's when we sense Him; that's when we see His gaze and feel the power of His endless fountain of love and redemption.

That gaze of our Savior—the gaze of both ultimate conviction and love. Think about how life-changing it really is. How many instances are there throughout the Gospels when Jesus turned His gaze on people, broken people who He then proceeded to heal both physically and spiritually with His astonishing gift of love?

Oh, and there were many who felt that wrath as well, right? Consider all those demons who were cruising along in so many people that came across Jesus' radar. One word—one gesture, and they scattered like cockroaches in bright sunlight.

And then there were all of those Pharisees and Sadducees. More than one of those guys had to be moved by His fire. This is not wishful thinking on my part!

No doubt, you've heard the phrase, "withering stare"?

That's probably an under-statement. No doubt His withering stare could reduce the arrogant to blubbering buffoons without a single word.

We can be certain how much He hates sin because it weighs down His beloved children and steals their destiny, causing lasting regret to say nothing of lost rewards. But not only does He want to protect us, He wants to crush sin and remove it once and for all from each of our lives because He wants nothing to stand between us and the grand and glorious plans He has for His beloved ones. And wouldn't we, like Him, do anything for our children?

But we must look at Him first, fixing our gaze on Him and never letting our eyes wander. Rather we are neither to give the enemy a single second of thought nor entertain any lie or temptation, ever! It's only there that we are safe, when we keep our eyes, like flint, on the goal of glorifying the Lord Jesus Christ with everything that's in us.

So turn to Him. Reach out to Him, feeling His warm embrace; experience the life-altering love He freely offers, and ask Him to help you see with the eyes of Heaven where the stumbling blocks are that you need to submit for His cleansing. There's nothing like it, and once you experience it, your life will forever change. You will be transformed by His love into that radiant bride for whom He died and will shortly return. Dear Friend, we will return to this subject of moving beyond your past later in this book. Please read on…

Look my way once again, dear Lord. Transform me by one look from your eyes! I long to see you and know you! I reach out and touch your face! Only you make me skip and dance for joy! Take me beyond my present experience and consume me with your love.

CHAPTER 8

His Bride Has Dove Eyes

Although her name may not be familiar to most, Hattie Philletta Hammond (1907-1994) was one of the leading evangelists of the early Pentecostal-holiness revival. She was born in Williamsport, Maryland and was a powerhouse, preaching a simple gospel message of relentless passion for Christ.

I want to share a little of her history, so you fully understand the impact of her story. She will be no stranger to you after you read this. She has inspired my life in so many beautiful ways. I have spent a great deal of time listening to her messages and reading what she left us.

From very early childhood Hattie was well aware of the call of God and initially planned to serve Him on the mission field. As a small child, her cousins would come to visit and enjoy playing church, converting and baptizing all the dolls in the neighborhood. When she had no other audience, she preached to the cows and chickens and to her own reflection in the mirror. At school she passed out gospel tracts and took a keen interest in the continent of Africa.

She contracted typhoid fever at the age of twelve, and because she wasn't expected to survive, her pastor was led to anoint her with oil and pray. It wasn't long before her 106-degree fever broke, and she regained her health.

Throughout her teenage years, though she loved God, she found church rather stuffy and would sneak off to do other things.

At age fifteen, she passed a large tent where Rev. John J. Ashcroft (grandfather of Senator John Ashcroft) was holding evangelistic services. It piqued her interest, so that she went inside and was gloriously converted and baptized in the Holy Spirit.

From that moment on she became a passionate soul winner, preaching in her high school to anyone who would listen. She'd lost her former shyness and had little interest in things of the world. At age sixteen she gave her life to full-time ministry as a traveling evangelist.

Not long afterward, Rev. Ashcroft asked her to join him and his wife for evangelistic services in Martinsburg, West Virginia. Night after night he preached, with little in the way of results. Then, one night, he asked Hattie to preach.

Throughout the song service, she cried out to the Lord, and the Holy Spirit impressed her heart with the

Draw Me

Scripture in Galatians 3:1: **"O foolish Galatians, who hath bewitched you, that you would turn from serving the living God?"** She got up to preach, but instead of praying or preaching, she simply repeated that text over and over.

After the third reading, a woman ran to the altar and cried out in repentance for backsliding. Abruptly, the power of God filled the place and inspired a spontaneous resurrection in the neighborhood. Hattie's seventy-one-year ministry was off to a stunning start.

Following the Martinsburg meetings, Hattie was preaching at a church in Cleveland, Ohio when, once again, the power of God fell hard on the audience. From that time on, wherever she went, amazing healing miracles occurred. Consequently, she grew to become known as "the girl evangelist" while she was still in curls. In 1927, she was ordained by the Assemblies of God and received invitations to speak in major cities all over the United States, preaching at conferences and conventions among Full Gospel circles as well as overseas.

By the 1930s, she was one of the most highly effective Bible teacher/evangelists in the Pentecostal movement, often preaching at large camp meetings. Her message was uncomplicated, encouraging total abandonment to the things of the Spirit. Ultimately, she inspired a deeper walk of holiness that had a huge impact on the culture of her day.

Her message was not an easy one to hear, calling believers to submit to the refining process of God, that is much like the making of fine wine. Just as He came to Earth to become broken bread and poured out wine, He takes us through crushing, milling and other hard places so that, together with other crushed grapes, we become one with Him and each other, losing our identity in exchange for His. In fact, we may often feel like we've had the very life crushed out of us, as an offering, a sweet sacrifice, which, in the end, is exactly His intention.

In 1981, Hattie spoke at the Fredericksburg Assembly of God, where the Spirit of God moved fresh and many were transformed by His mighty power. It was clear that her anointing was from God and not of men.

In the August 18, 1928 issue of the *Pentecostal Evangel* she wrote these words in an article entitled "Drawing Nigh Unto God": "As we enter into the presence of the Lord we should realize we are in the presence of a great, almighty, eternal God." She encouraged readers to rest in the presence of God and wait for Him to speak to them. She went on, "We should not rush into His presence with haste, nor come as though we were coming into the presence of an earthly friend. We should take time to realize that He is God and beside Him there is none else."

In this sermon she also spoke of the need for personal salvation, conscecrated times of prayer, and the importance of baptism in the Holy Spirit. She taught and modeled the importance of becoming still and knowing that God is the Great I Am to whom we owe great honor and a deep sense of respect. She felt strongly that we must invite the Holy Spirit to keep us true to the cross and to the Person of Jesus and to learn to truly choose to stay the course, no matter what the cost.

Her devoted life and preaching left a mark that is rarely seen anywhere. Even today, her example speaks volumes to convict those who have left their first love. In light of these truths it behooves each of us to examine our hearts for evidence that we've chosen to stay that same course, no matter what, because it will take that kind of passionate commitment in all of us to win the world for Christ.

Hattie shares a story in which she was once warned about speaking in a particular church. "Don't go there—no one comes out to special meetings," they boldly proclaimed. Hattie took this matter to the Lord and felt a clear witness to go anyway. The day of the meetings came and, sure enough, only a few older saints sat in the pews. The emptiness of the giant auditorium created a deafening silence that no one could ignore.

Hattie did what she did every meeting—she called on the name of her Jesus. If you ever heard Hattie preach, you'd know that when she said His name—JESUS—she spoke with such intimacy and hunger that it invited the instant presence of God. **The Lord came running when Hattie came calling. They were dear friends.**

Suddenly, from the back of the church, Hattie looked up and saw the Lord Jesus Christ enter the sanctuary through the door. She saw Him physically walk up the aisle, one-by-one passing the people who sat in the pews. His face was beautiful; His majesty was something to behold. Every inch of that church was filled with the tangible presence of Christ Himself. Hattie announced that Jesus was present and the people were moved beyond what words could possibly describe. After such a breathtaking encounter, hearts of listeners were stirred with desperation for deeper intimacy with the Lord.

The people who attended that night were so moved by the fact that Jesus was their honored guest that they told everyone what happened. The rest of that conference attracted crowds the church could barely contain. What made the difference? **A personal visit from a personal Christ. A supernatural hunger that compelled the Lord to come and rest in a church that night!** When we hunger for Jesus, really hunger for Him, He will come and abide in such a place. We may not see Him with our natural eyes as Hattie did that night, but He will come and dwell in such a people or place that desires Him. Hattie Hammond had dove eyes for her Bridegroom, and, even today, a deep hunger for God compels us to run after Him.

He Calls You, Beloved, into a Far Deeper Relationship with Him

"Behold, you are fair, My love! behold, you are fair! You have dove's eyes" (Song of Solomon 1:15).

In the same way He called Hattie to draw near, He calls you, Beloved, into a far deeper relationship with Him to focus your gaze on Him alone. Even as a dove fixes its gaze upon its mate, unmoved by distractions, even so, He wants you, His 'love bird' to focus on Him alone.

Scripture commands us not to be like a horse or a mule easily distracted by side vision. It can only be kept on track by placing 'blinders' beside each eye and a bit in its teeth.

Unlike the horse or mule, stubborn and easily distracted, your Bridegroom wants you to be like that 'love bird' with singular purpose, focusing dove eyes on Him so He can lead you according to His will.

Love Him enough to be obedient, allowing your spirit to become ever more sensitive to His still, small voice. He will lead you to safety, shelter, and protection—only trust Him and allow Him to guide your steps. Stay close enough to Him to sense His will for you. With one tender glance He will send you in the right direction, where you will find favor and spiritual substance.

"I will instruct you and teach you in the way you should go; I will guide you with My eye" (Psalm 32:8).

As your '*dove eyes*' focus on your Heavenly Bridegroom He will bring a greater awareness of His presence. He will begin to minister to you in a very personal way and lift you far above the pull of this evil world, giving you a new sensitivity to His Spirit.

How much do you love Him? Can He trust you to develop a singular focus on Him alone, even as Hattie had, so that you don't miss His best? Will you gaze upon Him only, leaving behind all others and the things that so tantalize you now? Once you fall in love with His face, you'll no longer be satisfied to merely hear *about* Him; rather you'll yearn for His presence, eager to be in His company where He will satisfy the deep longings inside you.

With that 'singular gaze' will also come a change in your desires. He will quench your cravings for the things of this world and inspire you to come away with Him.

Rise Up

"Rise up, My love, My fair one, and come away" (Song of Solomon 2:10).

He yearns for you to have only one desire—to abide in His holy presence. He longs for you to stay in His presence and never leave, no matter what else occupies your time.

Cry out even as David:

"The Lord is my light and my salvation; whom shall I fear? ... ***one thing have I desired of the Lord***, **that will I seek after; that I may dwell in the house of the Lord all the days of my life, to behold the beauty of the Lord, and to inquire in His temple"** (Psalm 27:1-4).

As you let Him stir your passion for Him, getting back to your first love, He will supply every need, filling you to overflowing and far surpassing your expectations—finally giving you that elusive deeper abundant life.

"But seek ye first the Kingdom of God and His righteousness; and all these things shall be added unto you" (Matthew 6:33).

Today, He searches earnestly for those who are willing to be doves with that kind of singleness of vision. When He finds them, it brings Him incredible joy, so that He can't help but declare:

"Behold, you are fair, you have dove's eyes" (Song of Solomon 1:15).

Once He knows you love Him most, more than great wealth, more than any other—once He has become to you a sought-after pearl of great price, He will be your fairest of ten thousand. He is altogether lovely, for He is your King of Kings and Lord of Lords, your All in All. Then, just as He did with Hattie, let Him bring you to the banqueting house where His banner over you is love!

Take me to your banqueting house! Ravish me with your love and tender affection. I give you all my heart; call me away into the deep, for you are altogether lovely!

CHAPTER 9

Rise up and Come Away

"Then as I looked, I saw a door standing open in heaven, and the same voice I had heard before spoke to me like a trumpet blast. The voice said, 'Come up here, and I will show you what must happen after this'"
(Revelation 4:1 NLT).

As previously mentioned, I meant this work to be a simple roadmap for those who want to go deep and have all of God they can get. Rather than lecturing, I want you to feel like you've sat down with a friend over coffee, one who encourages you to go higher in His presence. We know that His return is imminent, and, because that's so, He's asking His Bride—you and me personally, as well as the church, to rise up. But the truth is that not all of the church is listening. I've mentioned before that in every church you'll find two distinctive groups. There's the **church at large** and there's the **church within the church—the invisible church within the visible church.**

There's the church that is known by man and there's the church that's known only by God. And whether we see it or not, I'm convinced that there's always a remnant—a core group within every church that desperately wants more of Jesus. They're hearing and responding to the call to draw nearer to the Father's heart. Can you hear the call as you read? The Father is calling His Bride—wooing her to come away with Him, to rise above the distractions, to shake off the things that weigh her down, to come away with the Lord.

During one particular season there were many nights when the Lord would come for me and I can remember for a season of a year at least the Lord would often come to me at night, and He would say, **"Come away with Me, my love."** I sensed the very manifest presence as He entered my room.

He was asking me to **rise up.** And today He's asking the church to rise and come away into the secret place. And while many within the church can't even hear the call to come, the remnant has ears tuned to hear and respond to every word Abba says. I'm completely convinced that, in these end times, He's calling His people to rise up and get to know Him from a more deeply intimate place.

In Revelation Chapter 4, John heard the call to come higher. Then a door opened, and through it he heard the call to come up to a deeper dimension of fellowship than we've ever known before.

There Are Always Distractions in Every Life

I've been a Christian since I was five years old! Almost 42 years now! Both my father, grandmother, and grandfather were all pastors, so I'm a third-generation pastor on both sides of my family. I like to say that I've been in church since nine months before I was born! And I remember being in service after service where I had no motivation to change. One week led to another, and another, until it was New Years eve, when we began to reflect on our relationship with Christ and whether we had grown closer or further apart.

There are always distractions in every life, and that was certainly true of me. I had things to do and places to go, and there was little in the way of radical change, though I always had the best of intentions. But the days are over when we can simply go do the next thing and never get serious about our walk with the Lord. We have only to listen to the nightly news to realizing that we're living in treacherous times. It's also clear that the enemy has pulled out all the stops, knowing his time is short, to derail us from our eternal destiny and the will of God we are to live out while we're here. We need to be able to clearly hear the call of God and learn to obey for our own best interests and the interests of those around us, who are dancing on the edge of Hell with no idea what's on the other side.

Now is the time. Not next week. Not next month. The time is now! Right now, the Lord is wooing His church to come up, to rise to that higher place where you've never been before. You see, within your spirit there's a yearning that's never been understood, and it's time to allow yourself to yearn after God. Many of us make excuses for staying right where we are, saying, "Well, Lord, my spirit is willing but my flesh is weak." Now is the time to crucify the flesh and yield. Now is the time to rise up! This is the moment! Don't let it pass unnoticed.

We can't waste another year. We have to listen and respond to that call to come because within that call is spiritual substance and a revelation that He wants to download into our spirits. There's something so sweet about keeping company with the Lord. He comes to you and He enlarges your capacity to grasp the secrets of His heart, and He tells you to rise up because He has precious things to share with you. And then He begins to whisper in your ear, whispers from the throne room. (See my book *Whispers from the Throne Room* for more.) And you begin to grasp the big picture from His point of view. Your spirit grows stronger so that the fire of your love can't be extinguished.

Woo me to that higher place found only in you! Today is the day I run hard after you! I choose to rise up and yield to your perfect will. I will come away and push aside any distraction that I may make you the object of my affection!

CHAPTER 10

Forgetting Those Things That Are Behind

In Philippians 3:13, the second part of the verse says:

"...forgetting those things which are behind and reaching forth under those things which are before."

This is a living message to the church right now. We're in a place where we need to forget those things behind us and look ahead to what the Lord wants us to do and where the future is incredibly bright. If you have a past you're ashamed of, and Satan harasses you about it and tells you you're worthless to God, it's time to forget those things which are behind and press on toward the mark of the high calling.

I know whereof I speak because I, too, have experienced rejection and deep wounds that left me unable to function. In fact, I've written part of my story in my book called *Crocodile Meat*, but the point is I've come close to losing my life over a dozen times. While growing up I faced mass rejection and had absolutely no hope for the future. To be frank, I had every reason to be numbered among those who commit suicide.

And the pain didn't stop as I grew up. I faced an overwhelming number of trials in my adult life, because: **"Man is born out of trouble as the sparks fly upward,"** as Job said long ago (Job 5:7). Of course, some of those troubles were of my own making, while other times I was a victim of circumstance. As human beings we all face trouble, and it can take us into a downward spiral until we're in a place where we're focused on our trials and our regrettable past, so that we can't possibly hear God's voice or focus on His call to rise up and tune our ear to the Spirit.

At that point we're so obsessed with our past that the Lord is releasing this prophetic word over us: **"Hear the word of the Lord! In this moment it's time to forget those things which are behind! I don't condemn you. There's no condemnation to those that are in Christ Jesus. I will never throw your sins in your face. I don't bring them up because they're forgiven and forgotten, so you must cut the ties that hold you captive to old, dead things that poison your soul and hinder the glorious future I have for you."** Instead of living in victory, our old nature and the Devil send us right back into the cycle of guilt and shame, but it's time to stop the cycle and decide to believe what God says about us in His Word.

How to Overcome Your Past

I'm going to dedicate this larger chapter to the thought of overcoming your past because I believe it's impossible to truly embrace intimacy as His Bride if you have chains of yesterday's bondage dragging and holding you captive. Journey with me, precious one...

In Philippians 3:10-14 it reads, **"That I might know him, and the power of his resurrection, and the fellowship of his sufferings. Being made conformable unto his death; If by any means I might obtain unto the resurrection of the dead. Not as though I had already attained, either were already perfect: but I follow after, If that I may apprehend that for which I am apprehended of Christ Jesus. Brethren, I count not myself to have apprehended: but this one thing I do, Forgetting those things which are behind, and reaching forth unto those things which are before. I press toward the mark for the prize of the high calling of God in Christ Jesus."**

Paul had every reason not to become intimate with Christ and change his world. He was a killer of Christians, a murderer influenced by false religious doctrine. He referred to himself as "chief of all sinners." (1 Timothy 1:15 b). From man's perspective he had no right to ever call himself a Christian. But Abba was faithful to forgive him and use him mightily in ministry. This murderer-turned-apostle wrote over half of the New

Testament. For Paul to be useful to God, he had to put the tormenting images of his past behind him and move forward. I'm sure Satan seized every opportunity to remind him of his past sin. Paul had to choose not to entertain those thoughts but move on. He didn't let his past stop him, and neither should you!

Many people cannot positively impact their world, due to the pull of their past, because they believe the many lies of Satan. You must realize God wants to place His power and anointing within you and powerfully use you to invade the darkness regardless of your past. Many of you reading this are functioning far below par because you refuse to let go of your past. You haven't received Father's complete forgiveness. You don't believe Jesus will forgive you. You may say, "I believe that if I confess my sins He will forgive me," but, deep in your heart, you haven't truly believed Abba has forgiven you. You may also consider your sin(s) too big for Father to erase. You may even have repented of that same sin five minutes ago. How does Father forgive us? It's only by His grace and mercy. God's grace—His unmerited favor—is so hard to understand at times, but, thankfully, His grace is always there for us. (2 Cor. 1:3)

Because of the cross, Father will forgive you as much as He's willing to forgive me or anyone else. Abba doesn't have some big scale up in Heaven weighing how big your sin is to determine whether or not He will forgive you. No, Father forgives all sin when we sincerely repent. All sin is like indelible ink. The stain won't come out by any natural means. The only way the stain of sin can be removed is by the blood of Jesus. His blood can remove any sin no matter how big and dark the stain. Realizing this promise and not accepting Father's forgiveness for your sins is like stepping on the cross of Christ. What you're actually saying is, "Jesus, what you did on the cross is not good enough for me because my sin is special and I'm an exception to the rule." If this is your attitude, precious one, God desires to set you free. Will you let Him?

Did you know you can actually stifle the power and holy anointing God has placed within you by not excepting His forgiveness? It won't flow through you as it should because your eyes are focused upon yourself and not fixed upon God. The power of God only flows when you're focusing God-ward not self-ward. Another trap Satan employs is to try to turn you aside from the right path by getting your eyes off the road. He accomplishes this by throwing your past in your face, hoping you'll wallow in your problems rather than be used of God. Don't be ignorant of Satan's tactics. (2 Cor. 2:11) Self-centeredness is like a dam holding you back. Allow the blood of Jesus to destroy that dam. Let Holy Spirit power flow through you to its fullest potential. Satan's main goal is to destroy your faith and love toward Abba by telling you lies. (See John 8:44 and John 10:10) Choose this very day not to believe them. Instead, believe what God has to say because it's the truth, and that truth will set you free! (See John 8:32)

The Lord laid upon my heart five keys that will help His Bride get free from the past. If you struggle with your past or you struggle to accept God's forgiveness, take these five keys and begin to put them into practice in your life. Stand back and see what God will do!

Key Number One: Ask God for a Revelation of the Blood.

If you have a true revelation, which means you have an unveiling of the truth, or you see something in a fresh, new way, you'll be set free from the past. If you could truly understand what Jesus went through for you on the cross, I believe you would unreservedly accept Father's forgiveness for your past deeds. Just think about this for a moment.

Jesus left a glorious heaven

Jesus was confined to an earthly body

Jesus related to mankind completely

Jesus volunteered to pay the price for their sin

(Phil. 2:7-8)

He lived on this Earth for thirty-three years and died a terrible death for us. Let me describe for you all that Jesus went through for you at Calvary, so you may never again consider if Jesus truly loves you and is willing to forgive all sin.

Father's all-consuming love for us was decisively demonstrated at the cross. Isaiah 53:10 says it pleased the Lord to bruise Jesus and give Him grief. God let His love for mankind overcome and surpass His feelings of grief for His Son. Even knowing the brutal and most excruciating way Jesus would carry the sins of the world, God still allowed His Son to be the atoning sacrifice for the world—for us!

I don't think most Christians realize what Jesus went through for them. People often picture this "wimpy" looking Jesus on a cross with a few scratches on Him. What a terrible misconception. Jesus had a human body just like you and me. He felt pain just as we do. When He was hung upon the cross, He didn't even look like a man. He was so bruised and bloody that His features were unrecognizable. (Isaiah 52:14)

Crucifixion was the Roman death penalty for non-citizen slaves, foreigners, and criminals. It was the most agonizing and dishonorable death a brutal and barbarous empire could devise. Nails were driven through the hands and feet to a wooden cross. The victim was left hanging for days in complete agony, suffering both starvation and unquenchable thirst.

Crucifixion was not the only painful thing the Lord had to endure for us. He was whipped beforehand with a whip called the "cat-of-nine-tails". It was the Roman tool of choice for torture. Made up of nine strands of strong, thick leather cord, laced with pieces of metal, rock, wood and other sharp objects, it would literally rip the victim to shreds. Each time the whip reached its victim, it would literally wrap around the body. At that time the captors would pull it. This action would cause a breaking of arteries and veins, plus a ripping away of anything in its path, such as eyes. Many times, the prisoner would not survive the flogging. Jesus was whipped by soldiers over thirty times. All through this savage flogging, He never once cursed the soldiers. After His whipping, all that was left of Jesus was one massive piece of torn flesh.

But that's not all! Upon His head was slammed a crown of thorns. The length of each individual thorn was two to four inches—long enough to cause plenty of damage. Jesus must have suffered unimaginable pain as that crown was brutally shoved on His head by the soldiers.

And as if that wasn't enough, He was forced to drag a heavy cross to the Place of the Skull (Matt. 27:33), also known as Calvary or Golgotha. (Matt. 27:33). It took a real man to go through what Jesus did. Not some weak and skinny little Jesus but a big, strong man with a heart full of love for us.

Jesus was mocked, scoffed at, and jeered by the chief priests, elders, scribes, and soldiers. He faced a hard-hearted, contemptible crowd that wanted Him dead more than anything else. The Roman garrison with about five to six hundred men all joined in with the mockery and torment of Jesus. They hit Him. They spat upon Him. They even yanked out His beard.

He was very much battered while He accepted His fate. He supported a cross and wore the crown down a long, hard road—a road lined with merciless people who spat and mocked Him. Only a small crowd wept for Jesus. But He silenced them, saying, **"Weep not for me, but for your children."** (Luke 23:28) In Matthew 27:25, the crowd cried out, **"His blood be on us and our children."** To this day the blood of Jesus is still crying out because of the curse they brought down on themselves.

When Jesus reached the place of His crucifixion, they offered Him wine mixed with gall, to stupefy Him before the long nails were driven into His hands and feet. Jesus refused the gall. The nails that were driven into Him sent convulsions of excruciating pain into His nervous system.

The throbbing pain that Jesus felt was unbearable, and the long hours of torture that followed were incredible. It was an unimaginable trial to suffer thirst, starvation, breathing disorders, loss of blood, and the body slowly shutting down. Each time He would take a breath He would have to push with His legs, and pull His body upward, causing great pain throughout His body. Many times, a prisoner wouldn't have the energy to pull himself up to breathe and would die from suffocation. For this reason, the legs of the victims were broken to hasten death from lack of air. Death usually followed in four to six days. In Jesus' case, it spanned six hours. He was already dead when the spear pierced His side. Some medical authorities have said that when heart rupture occurs, blood collects in the pericardium (the lining around the heart) and often will divide into a watery curium. If this is true, then the reason for Jesus' death was heart rupture. Under extreme pain, and the pressure of His wildly racing blood, His heart burst. Darkness fell from noon to three that symbolized the way Abba turned His back on Jesus.

We plainly see the extent Father went through for mankind, allowing His only Son to die in such a way that He might be raised from the dead for mankind to be saved. Jesus had to drink the cup of death in our place. His blood was shed instead of ours.

Now let me ask you a question. Would a Father who sent His Son to die for a lost world in the most excruciating manner stop caring for His children? Would He refuse to forgive the very people for whom His Son died? Of course not! Abba's love for mankind is seen through the cross. Our God is a loving heavenly Father who desires to wipe away all your past. Abba, out of the very essence of His nature, never abandons us or flaunts our sin in our face but is there to forgive whoever will ask. His mercy is new every morning! (Lam. 3:22-23) So today ask Him for a revelation of Jesus' blood and cross, and move on from your past. Father is willing and able to forgive you, so accept His forgiveness.

Key Number Two: Forgive Yourself for Your Past.

One of the hardest things to do is to forgive yourself for your past. Sometimes you have no problem with accepting Father's forgiveness, but forgiving yourself is another story. You may feel as if you cannot live with yourself because of your past. Many people today are still beating themselves up for sins they committed years ago. They can't understand how in the world they could commit such a sin. They may even have made the same mistake time after time and refuse to believe they can change, so they don't forgive themselves. The bottom line is that Abba wants you to forgive yourself. If you truly want to be used of God with power and boldness, you must forgive yourself. I plead with you if you don't want the past to control you, please forgive yourself!

When you rehearse and torment your mind with past sins, you are opening the door to Satan. It's as if you are telling the Devil, "I enjoy having you around!" Unforgiveness gives Satan a foothold in your life. Father's blessing cannot be upon you when you refuse to forgive yourself. Kick the Devil out! Declare the blood of Jesus over your mind. The Devil has only one goal, to remind you of your past, so refuse to entertain any thoughts when he comes to harass you. Tell the Devil to take a hike because it's all under the blood! Remind the Devil of his future. Remember that when you stand before the Lord there is nothing to fear because you are forgiven. (1 John 4:18) Father sees the blood of Jesus when He looks at you. The blood covers your imperfections. It's as if Abba put on blood sun shades and only sees Jesus, so refuse to be frightened but forgive yourself and remind the Devil of this truth. This truth alone will send him running in terror! (James 4:7)

Key Number Three: Forget Your Past.

It's impossible to be bold for God when you repeatedly play your past in the theater of your mind. The more you play it the more you'll feel condemned. Romans 8:1 says, **"Therefore, there is now no condemnation for those who are in Christ Jesus, because through Christ Jesus the law of the Spirit of life set me free from the law of sin and death."** The Spirit never brings condemnation on a believer, but brings loving conviction to the heart. Hebrews 12:5-11 says, **"My son, do not make light of the Lord's discipline, and do not lose heart when he rebukes you, 6) because the Lord disciplines those he loves, and punishes everyone he accepts as a son. 7) Endure hardship as discipline; God is treating you as sons. For what son is not disciplined by his father? 8) If you are not disciplined (and everyone undergoes discipline), then you are illegitimate children and not true sons. 9) Moreover, we have all had human fathers who disciplined us, and we respected them for it. How much more should we submit to the Father of our spirits and live! 10) Our fathers disciplined us for a little while as they thought best; but God**

disciplines us for our good, that we may share in his holiness. 11) No discipline seems pleasant at the time, but painful. Later, however, it produces a harvest of righteousness and peace for those who have been trained by it."

The work of the Holy Spirit is to correct, but He never does it to discourage or destroy. Condemnation always brings people down, rather than build them up. John 10:10: **"The thief (Satan) comes to kill steal and destroy; I come that they may have life, and have it to the full."** Satan's threefold plan for your life is to steal, to kill you and to ultimately destroy you. One way he does this is through condemnation. The Holy Spirit always convicts because this brings life and not death! Yes, God's correction can hurt at times, but it's always done out of love and not to leave a person feeling worthless and hopeless.

Condemnation = Judgment not based on love, but is meant to push down

Conviction = Correction from God that builds up

Repeatedly replaying your past in the theater of your mind will only let condemnation creep into your life. Forgetting your past is only possible by accepting God's forgiveness and moving on. You cannot drive down the road while looking in your rearview mirror, and you can't go through life being consumed by your past. It reads in Micah 7:19, **"He will turn again, he will**

have compassion upon us; he will subdue our sins." What does the word "subdue" mean? To subdue something means we beat it down, we get rid of it; we diminish it or smash it. The Bible is saying that God takes all our sins and smashes them up and destroys them and throws them into the sea. Cory ten Boom put it this way: "God takes all our sins and throws them into the deepest ocean and puts a big sign that says, 'No Fishing.'" Don't be like so many Christians who ask forgiveness but keep going back to that sea with their fishing rod and take back everything they just gave to God.

Satan also loves to send you into depression and the depths of despair. So many times, when I get down, I throw myself a pity party and sing that song my mom used to joke about: "Nobody likes me; everybody hates me; I guess I'll go eat worms." The problem is that we really don't eat those worms; we go fishing with them in the sea of forgetfulness. Stop fishing in your past and playing those old films and start renewing your mind with the Word of God and His promises. Stop putting junk into your mind about all your past defeats; this will only stifle the power of God flowing through you. Romans 12:2 tells us, **"Do not conform any longer to the pattern of this world, but be transformed by the renewing of your mind; then you will be able to test and approve what God's will is—his good, pleasing and perfect will."** Transforming the mind by reading the Word and carefully replacing negative thoughts with positive things that God says will transform your mind. Philippians 4:8 says, **"Finally, brothers, whatever is true, whatever is noble, whatever is right, whatever is pure, whatever is lovely, whatever is admirable—if anything is excellent or praiseworthy—think about such things."** There are great teaching CDs and wonderful anointed preaching videos that will minister to you and help renew your mind. Also, we have countless Christian books available to read. Personally, I think that the more you read the Holy Word, and even some other Christian books, the stronger your spirit will become. Let me encourage you to wash your mind with the Word. I promise you won't regret it!

Number Four: Forgive Those Who Hurt You.

Many times, getting free from our past can be difficult because other people have caused severe pain. Has someone deeply hurt you? If you refuse to forgive, you drag that person through life with you. You can only be released from the control of that person when you forgive them. The word "forgive" means to give something. You're giving that person freedom from being indebted to you. You then receive peace in your heart.

In Ephesians 4:32

"Instead, be kind and merciful, and forgive anyone who does wrong, just as Christ has forgiven you. Love is more important than anything else. It is what ties everything completely together."

If we expect God to forgive our sins (we all sin and fall short of His glory) - (**Romans 3:23**) then we too must forgive and forget. We only hurt ourselves when we refuse to forgive. We're the ones who lose in the end if we fail to let go of an offense. Unforgiveness always turns to bitterness, and if not dealt with, it leads to destruction. The Lord will not have an angry, sour, bitter Bride!

Number 5: Embrace Father's Forgiveness and Let Him Set You Free.

The effects of the past can only be changed through Jesus Christ, who desires to set us all free from the past. You can begin by:

- Asking God for a fresh discovery of the blood.
- Forgiving yourself.
- Forgetting the past.
- Forgiving others who have hurt you.
- Embracing God's forgiveness and letting Him set you free.

Take some time for personal reflection before we continue this journey together and pursue intimacy with our Bridegroom:

- Have you made a fresh discovery of the blood of Jesus?
- Have you forgiven yourself from your past mistakes?

- Do you continue to criticize yourself for your past?
- Do you play reruns of your mistakes in your mind?
- Have you released others who've hurt you?
- Do you embrace Father's forgiveness every day and know you're special to Him?
- How do you perceive Father's attitude toward you after you ask forgiveness?

Conclusion: God is good, and His mercy endures forever—that's a promise from God's Word. It also says He forgives everyone who repents. So who are we to hold on to the things God has not only forgiven but forgotten? When we fail to forgive others or ourselves, we undermine and often forego the blessings and wonderful future He has for us. *In fact, the only thing Father can't do is override your will in these situations.* So now's the time to take stock and see what's been holding you back, robbing you of your destiny. I promise you'll never be the same again.

Lord, I refuse to allow my past to steal my heart or my intimacy with you. I leave the past in the past. I embrace you and seek you with all my heart for a fresh, new encounter! Oh, Abba, I must have you! Nothing compares to you, nothing in my past can tear me from your loving embrace. I run to meet you now ... for you have been waiting for me with your tender affections.

CHAPTER 11

Deep Healing and God's Secrets

I had to come to the place where I cut loose from the old things that haunted me and accepted Father's deep healing so I could focus on what He had to share with me. At that point He welcomed me into His presence so He could show me the awesome future ahead.

Did you know that the Lord has secrets He wants to share with you? The thing is that He only shares His secrets with His closest friends. (Psalms 25:14) Once I said to Him, "Lord, what's on your heart right now?" I'd spent so much time telling Him my problems that I'd neglected to give a thought to what was on His heart. Now, I'm not saying that it's wrong to pray about our issues, because Scripture says (1 Peter 5:7) we're to cast all our cares on Him for He cares for us, but perhaps it's time to start bearing His burdens as well.

So I said, "Lord, is there something right now that's breaking your heart? Is there something that you'd like to share with me? I ask because it occurs to me that a friend shares and bears the burdens of a friend, and I've never done that for You." Have you ever had a friend in the natural realm that did all the talking and didn't seem to want to hear what you had to say? It was always about them…

When you went to lunch together, they did all the talking while you wished you could say something, but that moment never came. Or you'd get about halfway through a sentence when they interrupted. Have you ever had a friend like that? Well, sometimes we're that way with the Lord. The Lord can't even get a sentence out because we're so busy talking and talking. And sometimes I think the Lord says, "Shhh . . . be still and know that I am God."

When We Finally Quiet Our Hearts Before the Lord

Sometimes the Lord must remind me of what David said, **"I waited quietly before the Lord"** (Psalms 62:1). When we finally quiet our hearts before the Lord, He will begin to share what's on His heart. When I asked Him what was on His heart, He said child pornography, child abuse and abortion were weighing heavy on His heart. I was blown away at His response, and those burdens became my burdens as well, like a download from

Heaven. If you're an intercessor you know what I'm talking about, where the Lord will download you with the burden so that you'll wrestle in prayer over it, weeping over it in prayer. In this case, I was weeping and wrestling in prayer for some time before I realized I was actually fellowshipping with the Lord in His sufferings.

As His Bride, we can fellowship with the Lord both in His joys and in His sufferings, those things that are heavy on His heart. When I asked what was on His heart, He mentioned three specific things that grieved Him. I wept on my face for hours and then finally it lifted, and I realized I had prayed clear through until the burden lifted. At that moment He revealed that there are very few people who will do that, and I realized that I was humbled to be one of them. Prior to that moment I was so busy running into my prayer closet, sharing all my needs, that I never stopped to wonder if He had things He wanted me to intercede for or burdens He wanted to express. The stunning truth is that He will reveal His secrets to you, and those things will absolutely change your life. He'll give you a personal revelation and allow the Word of God to come alive as you rise up and listen to what He has to say. We're all familiar with the verse that says, **"I press on toward the mark for the prize of the high calling of God in Christ Jesus."** (Philippians 3: 14) Note that it doesn't say *I coast*. It says *I press*. There's a pressing, there's a resistance. It's not an easy quest.

Sometimes, while dealing with your own heartache and pain, you choose to press in toward the mark of the high calling of God. What is that high calling? The high calling is knowing Him—really knowing Him—well enough to hear His heart cry and praying for breakthroughs in those areas. Do you want to really know Him? Do you want to know Him enough to bear His burdens in prayer? Then listen and obey, casting aside all distractions and hindrances when He says to rise up in the moment and listen to the cries of His heart. I promise that, if you do that, not only will you discover deep healing but you'll never be the same again.

Heal me every place that I hurt. Take away the pain and make all things new! I embrace my healing, I embrace that perfect love that transforms me from the inside out!

CHAPTER 12

He Cometh Leaping upon the Mountains

Oh, how the Lord is calling His Bride to draw near! Revelation 19:7 tells us, **"Blessed are those that are called to the Marriage Supper of the Lamb."** And then it speaks about how she has prepared and made herself ready for His return. Oh, how the Lord is looking for a mature Bride who's ready and listening for His call to come. Oh, how the Lord is looking for a Bride who's mature!

Matthew 25 says He's searching for a Bride who will have her lamp trimmed and filled with oil. In the parable of the ten virgins, we must realize that the ten were not five Christians and five unbelievers. Nowhere in the Bible will you ever find an unbeliever described as a virgin. Virginity always speaks of purity. They were ten Christians; yet five were foolish and five were wise. We see that in every church today—both the foolish and the wise.

Sometime in the near future will come a time when the Lamb will return for His Bride. Will we be among the wise ones who have oil in their lamps, who are prepared, ready and eager for His return? Who of us will be alert, yearning for Him the way He yearns for us? What about you? Are you ready? Are you pushing aside the interferences? Are you rising up and following after Christ with all your heart? His eyes will blaze like fire as He walks to and fro, searching for someone who loves Him enough to rise up. He's searching for a Bride who's yearning, who's hungry and thirsty—desperate to be with Him. He urges those who are thirsty to come to the waters and drink. (Is. 55)

He's waiting for a Bride who's ready. He's not cruising the nursery looking for an immature, easily distractible bride. No, He's searching for a mature Bride who's willing to rise up and do whatever it takes to connect to her Beloved. Rise up. Song of Solomon 2:8 says, **"the voice of my beloved, behold he cometh leaping upon the mountains, skipping upon the hills."** Did you know that the Lord comes leaping and skipping in your direction? Doesn't that notion just melt your heart? I'm not talking about Jesus as a painting on a wall. I'm not talking about Jesus who's nothing more than a story in a book. I'm talking about Jesus your Heavenly Bridegroom who comes skipping at the very sound of your voice—a Bridegroom who eagerly anticipates joining His Bride!

Leaping upon the Mountains and Skipping upon the Hills

There's nothing that can stop a bridegroom from seeing his bride on their wedding day. He would scale the highest mountain or go through the deepest ditch; he'd leap over a bus if necessary. The Lord is no different; He wants to hold His Bride so He calls out to her with a loving, tremulous voice, leaping upon the mountains and skipping upon the hills, running in your direction to find you.

Again, scripture says, **"My beloved is like a gazelle or a young stag. Look! There he stands behind our wall, gazing through the windows, peering through the lattice."** (Song of Solomon 2:9) At this very moment your Bridegroom is standing and waiting behind the window lattice and He wants to know if you want Him.

You see, because He's a gentleman, He won't force Himself on anyone within His church. He won't run up and say, "Listen, buddy, like it or not, you're going to spend time with me." He'll stand behind the lattice, patiently waiting for our response. He'll wait and whisper, **"Come away with Me My Love, come away with Me"** (Song of Solomon 2:10, 8:14).

I often have visions of the Lord walking in my direction, waiting for me. Sometimes I've kept Him waiting because I didn't realize how much He yearned for my attention. I didn't treasure His call to come, to rise up. I got lost in distractions, taking Him for granted.

At times the Lord comes night after night for us, inviting us to rise up and come away. Then He patiently waits for our reaction. He has much to tell us that will change the very essence of who we are. And yet, until we grasp the treasure He offers us, we are never changed into His likeness. But He won't beg and plead for us to come. It's up to us. But will we accept His invitation or ignore it?

Winter is Past

Verse number ten of chapter 2 says, **"My beloved spake and he said unto me rise up my love, my fair one and come away."** I can't tell you how many times I've read that scripture. And I've often heard the Lord say those very words to me. "Rise up, my love, my fair one, come away." The Lord is calling His church to rise in this late hour. He's calling His Bride to hear verse 11: **"For lo the winter is past and the rain is over and gone and the flowers appear on the earth and the time of the singing of the birds is come and the voice of the turtle dove is heard in our land."**

Winter has passed, which means we are to forget those things which are behind us. So again, cut away the ties that hold you captive to the past season and keep you from knowing His presence. The Lord says prophetically, even now, "**that winter is past. You're in a new season. The barrenness is over; you're in a new season where you hear the singing of the birds, where there's a spirit of worship!**" You're worshiping the Lord in spirit and in truth. In this place, you can hear the voice of the turtle dove, which is His prophetic voice speaking into your life and where the Word of God comes alive like a two-edged sword, cutting away the old ways.

Right now, He's declaring to the church that winter (a time of spiritual apathy and deadness) is past, and He wants us to find deep healing and forget the past and focus on the future, where we listen and obey only what He says. It's time to listen to His call to rise up. The Lord Jesus is the uninvited guest who comes at inconvenient times to change us in ways we can't even imagine.

I can't tell you how many times I've been asleep in bed in that cozy little place where we all like to be, when all of a sudden the Lord would come and invite me to come away with Him. At that moment I had to make a choice to get up and sit with Him and let Him share His heart, taking me to a higher place, giving me fresh revelation or a present word from the Lord, or stay in my warm, cozy bed.

As much as I hate to admit it, I used to curl up in my bed and ignore His calls to come away with Him, even when He promised to use that time to set me free. Well, how did I know if it was the Lord waking me? That was my excuse, but the truth is that I don't wake myself at three in the morning, wondering if I should pray. Only the Lord does things like that, which is why I now often get up and pray. When was the last time you just woke up in the middle of night and wondered if you should pray? That's the Lord beckoning you to come. If you wake up in the middle of the night, get up and pray because the Lord is offering you something wonderful, something beautiful just for you.

Come leaping in my direction, my Heavenly Bridegroom, and wake me by the announcing of your presence! I feel you coming toward me now; I see your face; I feel the winds of refreshment... Do not turn away ... you are welcome in my life. Stay and dine with me for your love is better than wine!

CHAPTER 13

He Announced His Presence

I shared a story once in my book, *Whispers from the Throne Room*, of a season I was praying on May 5, 2006, when I suddenly saw a powerful prophetic inner vision of the Lord walking into my room and announcing His presence! I lay there stunned seeing His train fill the room. His power and presence were sweet when He said, **"Come away with Me, My love."** There was no way I could say no once I considered His brilliant loving eyes.

I followed Him into the living room and sat in my prayer chair. In the next instant the whole scene changed, and I was sitting in Heaven at a large table that extended as far as the eye could see, but only a handful of people sat at the table filled with platters of food covered with domed silver covers.

As I sat there, I immediately remembered the many times over the past few months when the Lord had called me and I had turned over and gone back to sleep.

Having said that, I want people to know this walk of intimacy has been a struggle, and not one in which I automatically obeyed, like a perfect saint of Christian living. But at that moment, I felt so ashamed that I fell down on my face before Him and wept over my disobedience. He lifted me up, looked into my eyes and said, "I don't even remember that anymore, because you repented, and turned things around." When I took my seat, I felt that awful guilt lift. I was free!

There's no condemnation for those that are in Christ Jesus because all their sins are covered by the blood. I'm not here to condemn or make anyone feel bad. I'm here to see The Lord breathe fresh intimacy into your heart because you and I are free and forgiven, and a bright, brilliant future lies ahead. No matter how often you've missed it, you probably weren't as disobedient as I was.

But I say these things so you'll learn to be obedient, so that you'll have a fresh desire to listen and heed that call to come up. At that moment the Lord walked toward the table and said, "Only a few of my choicest servants choose to get up in the night with Me." Then I knew that was why so few were gathered at the table. The sad truth is that the Lord had called many people but only a few joined Him during those long night hours.

Angels appeared and went around the table, removing the covers off the platters and filling plates with food. All those at the table had large helpings; my serving was noticeably smaller. I struggled to understand why.

Draw Me

The scene another time replayed in my spirit. Once again, when I sat in my favorite living room chair, the scene changed to the long dining table in Heaven. The scenes continued to repeat themselves, but each time the food was served my plate had a larger helping. Just before the vision ended, the food filled my plate.

Then the Lord spoke to my spirit. "As you're obedient to get up in the middle of the night to answer my call, I will give you more spiritual substance, more revelation, increasing your capacity to receive more."

Over the years, I've known and read the work of powerful pioneers in the faith like Wade Taylor, John Wright Follette, Walter Beuttler and Hattie Hammond, who, though they're now with the Lord, carried a lantern and impacted me by their deep dedication to intimacy with God.

Revelation 3:20 tells us, **"Behold, He stands at the door and he knocks."** The knock is the Lord calling you to rise up past the distractions and hear the Word of the Lord. He comes and knocks. This was written to the **church** of Laodicea.

Most of the time we hear this passage taught we think it's directed at unbelievers, but it was actually written to the lukewarm church. The Lord is still knocking on the door today. He's still asking His church to open the door so He can spend time with us. But are our ears tuned to hear what the Spirit is saying? Can we hear the knocks of the Lord? It's time to rise up and answer His call before it is too late.

A Heart That Is Awake

Song of Solomon 5:2 says this: **"I sleep but my heart is awake."** What does that mean? How can you be asleep while your heart is awake? It's something that happens when you're so in love with Jesus and so yearning that, even when your body is at rest, going to sleep, you say to the Lord, "Abba, even as I sleep I want my heart to be ready to hear if You speak."

When I began to pray that my heart would be open and burning before the Lord day and night even in my sleep, I noticed something. I would wake in the night and begin to prophesy. It wasn't a dream—I was sleeping. I wasn't thinking about anything in particular. I just woke up, sat up in bed and prophesied. Sometimes I began to speak in tongues. I was asleep, but my heart was awake!

The Lord is searching far and wide for a Bride who so yearns after Him that even when she's asleep she's awake to the Spirit realm. That lantern behind the lattice is still burning before the Lord. It indicates that even as I sleep my heart is awake. **"It's the voice of my beloved that knocketh saying open to me my sister, my love my dove, my undefiled for my head is filled with the dew and my locks with the drops of the night."** (Song of Solomon 5:2)

Let me share again of our Heavenly Bridegroom that goes to pursue His Bride, to the chambers, and knocks on the door with hair that's wet with dew. Again, why was His head wet with dew? Because He had previously visited many houses and knocked but they refused to answer the door. So with His head wet with dew He left that place and went elsewhere.

This is a prophetic revelation, seeing Him go to elsewhere for fellowship when He is refused admittance. He calls you His dove. In case you're not aware of it, a dove is a very special bird because it has tunnel vision; it only sees what's directly in front of it. It's not like a mule that sees what's on both sides of its head. The Lord says prophetically over you, "You're my dove, I see only you." But you know the profound thing is that I have all of Jesus to myself because He only sees me, but at the same time He only sees you. That's true of each of us.

I sense Him also saying, "You're my dove, and I've come for fellowship with you." Now, what does His Shulamite hostess do in the situation? His head is wet with dew when she says, **"I have taken off my coat. Why should I put it on again? I have already washed my feet; why should I defile them again?"** (Song of Solomon 5:3). In other words, she turned Him away after already washing her feet. Back then, they had roads and floors of dirt. She was saying that she had already washed up, and she didn't want to be inconvenienced or do it again. She was in that cozy, comfortable place. But after He left she realized that she would miss the hour of His visitation if she didn't run after Him and invite Him in.

She could smell the lingering scent of myrrh on the door handle, left by his hands. In the same way, there are times when the Lord will call out and invite us to come away with Him, and we turn Him away.

Then we, too, will realize what the Shulamite woman did and get up, only to learn it's too late to catch Him because He's already moved on. We can even smell the scent of His anointing on the door handle, but we've missed our hour of visitation. That's why it's so important that we listen and obey when the Lord calls us to rise up. Otherwise, we, too, will miss our hour of visitation.

I can testify of times when the Lord called me away from what I was doing, and when I rose to meet Him, He gave me such a powerful revelation that I began to share it around the world. As you can well imagine, that revelation was life-changing, so much so that I'm always grateful for that particular time we spent together. My plate was heaped high with manna from Heaven because I heeded His call to come away.

My Beloved Had Withdrawn Himself and Was Gone

In verse 6 it says, **"And I opened to my beloved but my beloved had withdrawn himself and was gone. My soul failed when he spake. I sought**

him but I could not find him. I called him but he gave me no answer." She was heartbroken realizing she'd missed her hour of visitation. I want to encourage you not to miss your hour with the Lord. When He calls out to you to spend time alone with Him, obey His wooing, for if you don't, you'll never know what you missed, but you can be sure it was a treasured gift.

In verse 8 we find that the Shulamite went to speak to the **Daughters of Jerusalem.** Now, the Daughters of Jerusalem are symbolic of the lukewarm Christian, the casual Christian, the status quo Christian who is a spectator of the deeper things going on in the inner sanctum of God, but they're not motivated to pay the price for entrance to that secret place. So she goes to the lukewarm ones and tells them she missed her opportunity and is desperate to find Him. And they respond, essentially saying, "What's the big deal? Why is this guy better than any other?" (See Song of Solomon 5: 9)

It will be obvious that your lukewarm friends will have no clue about the yearning in your heart for the deeper things of God. They don't understand why you want to shut off the television and go to your room to pray. They're confused when they see you skip a meal to fast and intercede. They have no idea why you guard your eye and ear gates from the dark things around you, but the Lord can use you to make a lasting impact even on the lukewarm Daughters of Jerusalem in your life if you let Him.

In verse 9 we read, **"What is your beloved more than any other? Oh, thou fairest among women, what is your beloved more than another beloved that you so charge us this way?"** So what's the big deal? Why are you so frantic about this guy?" And she answered, **"My beloved is white and ready. The chiefest among ten thousand. His head is as the most fine gold, his locks are bushy and black as ravens, his eyes are the eyes of doves by the rivers of water washed with milk and fitly set, his cheeks are as the bed of spices and sweet flowers, his lips are as the lily dropped into a sweet smelling myrrh, his hands are like the gold ring set with beryl. His belly is bright ivory overlaid with sapphires, his legs are pillows of barbell set upon the sockets of fine gold, his consonance is as Lebanon, excellent as the cedars, his mouth is most sweet, ye he is all together lovely. This is my beloved and this is my friend, oh Daughters of Jerusalem"** (Song of Solomon 5:10-16).

She responds, describing her beloved in such beautiful personal detail. She had spent time with him in his chambers. She heard the wooing of His heart. As Song of Solomon 1:4 says, **"Draw me and I will run after thee. The king has brought me into his chambers."** She has spent time with the king in his chambers and she received a profound revelation of who he is and the anointing that came with it.

So how did the Daughters of Jerusalem respond? Their response will probably make you speechless. **"Where is your beloved gone, oh thou amongst women? <u>Where is your beloved turned aside that we may seek Him with thee?</u>"** (Song of Solomon 6:1). Oh, isn't that precious? In other words, after they heard the personal account and saw that the bride was so enamored with him, they said, "Where is he? I want him too." This is why I want to encourage you in this deeper walk with the Bridegroom.

Some of you have been praying for your loved ones for a long time, but they're incredibly stubborn, unwilling to listen. Go get into your prayer closet and refuse to leave until you carry such a sweet anointing on your life that you will scarcely have to open your mouth before God comes through with a plan to answer you!

I listen and obey the calls to come away with you, Lord, because I am transformed in your presence; your scent will envelop me, and others will take note that I've been with you, Jesus, and they will want what I have and desire what I carry. May I lead them to you for everything I have comes by you alone!

CHAPTER 14

A Bride That Prepares

When you mention the Bride of Christ, many people are confused. Men especially can't relate to being a bride. I imagine the ladies struggle in the same way trying to relate to being a son of God, but the Bride and the Mature Son are two sides of the same coin.

We're called into maturity, to rise up and be ready as a company of overcomers. I believe the bride and the man child in the Book of Revelation refer to a remnant of believers who are numbered among the wise virgins of Matthew 25. They left behind long ago any semblance of Laodicean lukewarm Christianity. They're alert, wise and prudent, ready and prepared for His return with oil in their lamps.

Over the years I've met some who distort the message of the Bride, making it sound odd and flaky, while others make the relationship sound seductive and carnal. The love between us and the Lord is not sexual in nature but rather holy and pure, based on agape unconditional love.

Despite these issues, we can't throw the baby out with the bath water, believing the message of the Bride is wrong. I'm here to tell you that Jesus is looking for a mature Bride—us.

"Let us be glad and rejoice, and give him glory for the marriage of the lamb has come and his wife has made herself ready" (Revelation 19:7-9).

The Lord is anticipating a Bride who can't wait to get married—a Bride who can hear the call to come.

What kind of wedding would it be if the Bride was miserable on her wedding day and the groom acted like he didn't want to be there? That marriage would be doomed, but many people in the body of Christ don't realize that the wedding day is imminent, and they look much like that miserable Bride. If they're saved, they need to tell their face about it because they don't look like they're anticipating marriage to Christ, the Lover of their souls.

Now, if you have a picture-perfect spouse and you think your spouse is the most perfect person in the world, I guarantee that sometime during your marriage your spouse will disappoint you. But the perfect Gentleman, our Heavenly Bridegroom, never disappoints us. So if we're the mature Bride of Jesus Christ we should be prepared and excited, anticipating the day of the wedding. Rather than dreading that day, we need to say, "I am too blessed to be depressed. I can't wait for the wedding!"

The Wise and the Foolish

I mentioned Matthew 25 regarding the ten virgins, five wise and five foolish. This is a prophetic view of the church today because, in the same way, there are both foolish and wise Christians. The foolish ones twiddle their thumbs, completely absorbed by the things of this world. They don't realize that they're not ready for the return of Christ because they don't have the oil of the Holy Spirit at work in their lives, warning and equipping them for the future. We talked about the wise ones who occupy the secret place, unlike those spectators who are content to be in the outer court but never enter the inner court. The wise ones enter through the veil, hungering and thirsting for more of Him.

Now we see in verse 8: **"And to her was granted that she should be arrayed in fine linen, clean and white: for <u>the fine linen is the righteous acts of saints</u>."** As we noted earlier, we prepare ourselves to be that bride through our righteous acts and deep passion to hear and obey the call of God to draw near.

Verse 9 says, **"And he said to me, write, blessed are those who are called to the marriage supper of the lamb and he said to me, write these true sayings of God."** <u>Blessed are those who are called</u>. So if we've prepared ourselves, we're summoned by invitation to the Marriage Supper of the Lamb. What about you? Are you prepared? Do you have your invitation in hand or are you twiddling your thumbs saying, "I have my whole life to get things together"?

His Bride carries the manifest glory of God, a special presence that surrounds her wherever she goes. She is a carrier of the very atmosphere of Heaven. That means she's saturated with the same presence that's found in the throne room of God, resting in and upon her, so that dazzling brightness reflects on her face. The same glory that's integral in the throne room emanates from her at the deepest level.

I will dare to say again two classes of people have always populated the church—those who are prepared and those who are unprepared, content just to be saved. The second group says, "I'm happy as long as I make it to Heaven." They're the foolish virgins who don't personally know the Lord and are good with that. The first group includes the mature Bride of Jesus Christ. And because of that level of commitment to the Father, because they have saturated themselves in His presence, they're now carriers of the presence and maturity radiates from them as they go about doing their "righteous acts" as unto the Lord.

Revelation 19:8 says that through their righteous acts they're prepared for the Marriage Supper of the Lamb. It's sober to realize that both groups fill our churches. The Lord will say over these wise virgins, "Well done, thou good and faithful servants," and over the others He will say, "Well?" He couldn't possibly say, "Well done," if they've been apathetic or cold toward Him. In the church today we somehow have the idea that He's a big sugar daddy up the sky, and we can do whatever we want and never give an account for it one day. We will give an account. I say this only with pure love as I must speak the truth even if it is unpopular. I will be held accountable if I don't speak honestly.

I'm not saying that we should fear God with an unholy terror, but we should revere and respect Him, because He holds the key to our placement in eternity. We should stand in awe of Him and say, "God, I want to prepare myself. I want to live to please You only. I want to live a holy life. I know I'm unworthy but, Father, I want You to search my heart and if there be any wicked way within, create in me a clean heart." And I'm not going to waste my time feeling sorry for myself. Instead I'm going to rise up and say, **"Though He slay me, yet I will trust Him"** (Job 13:15).

And I'm not going to be miserable. I'm not going to be a secret undercover follower of Christ who looks just like everyone else. What does it say in Matthew 5? **"That they may see your good works and glorify your father which is in heaven."** (v.16) They should be able to perceive something different about you. They may not be able to explain it at first, but it shouldn't be long before they know you're a true Christ follower by the way you are. If they can't tell you're born again, then either you're a covert Christian or you fell off the wagon altogether. If we act just like the world, what kind of testimony is that? Who will be won to Christ if we're silent and sullen like the world? How can they see Jesus in us? There are certain places I won't go, certain things I won't do because it would sully my testimony before those who don't know Him. Did I make mistakes along the way? Yes, I made mistakes; we all fall short in some way, but a righteous man falls seven times and repents before he gets up and keeps going. (See Romans 3:23, Proverbs 24:16) The important part is to repent and learn from your blunders while pressing on toward the mark of the high calling! (See 1 John 1:9, Philippians 3:13, 14) I can't sugarcoat this message or water it down... Christ will have a Bride that prepares.

Lord, may I be found prepared for your coming. May I be awake to the deeper things of the Spirit! I refuse to give into the lukewarm spirit of this age! I will not be lulled to sleep, but I will arise and stir up the embers of passion within; I will trim my lamp and have fresh oil burning before your throne!

CHAPTER 15

The Preparation of a Queen

In this section we're going to consider what it means to count the cost of servanthood, the way the Bride of Christ must, and the way Queen Esther did.

In Esther 1:9 we read, **"At the same time Queen Vashti gave a banquet for the women in the royal palace of King Ahasuerus."**

Verse 10 says, **"And on the seventh day of the feast when the king Ahasuerus was in high spirits because of the wine, he told the seven eunuchs who attended him, and he named all of these people."**

Verse 11: **"To bring Queen Vashti to him with the royal crown on her head."** He wanted the nobles and all the other men to gaze on her beauty for she was a very beautiful woman.

Verse 12 goes on to say, **"But when they conveyed the King's order to Queen Vashti, <u>she refused to come</u>, this made the king furious and he burned**

with anger." There was a call for the queen to come before the king and Vashti decided that she didn't feel like it. What did the king do when the queen refused to come? He became irate, because nobody, but nobody was allowed to refuse a request from the king. Vashti is a type of the flesh, the willful, rebellious side of our human personalities.

Let me make it really simple using a visual example you've no doubt heard before: You have a little angel on one shoulder and a little Devil on the other shoulder. The little angel says, "Do this," and the little Devil says, "No. Do the exact opposite." Who are you going to listen to? Your spirit and your flesh are at war with each other. But who will win this battle? The one we've fed the most. The side we've nurtured and encouraged to go the distance.

The book of Galatians explains the war between the spirit and the flesh. When your flesh doesn't want to be told what to do, it cops an attitude. Does that sound familiar? Well, I've seen it especially in the workplace. Without speaking a word, you know they're silently saying, "Nobody is going to tell me what to do."

When your boss says I want you to do this, inside you're saying, *Nah! You're not going to tell me what to do!*

I've also seen it in the church when the pastor says, "Please don't bring drinks or chew gum in the sanctuary."

And inside you're saying, *Forget that. I'm going to sneak it in or keep my gum in my mouth. He won't know.*

Inside each of us, even passionate believers, is a rebel who is tempted to say, "Nobody is going to tell me what to do." The only way that changes is if we have trained our hearts to submit to the will of God and let Him control who we are and how we live.

The Submitted, Mature Bride of Jesus Christ

Right now, the Holy Spirit is calling the Bride to come unto Him, to go past the veil into the Holy of Holies and to do what's right, but your flesh, the "Queen Vashti" in you, doesn't want to do it. Your flesh, the rebellious side of you, hates the idea of becoming that submitted, mature Bride of Jesus Christ. Some people think, *Oh, that's no problem. That's easy.* No, it's not. It's not easy to conform to the image of Christ, it's not easy to "crucify the flesh." It's not easy to tell the little Devil on your shoulder, "I'm not going to do that." It's not easy to pick up your cross and follow hard after Him.

Consider this: If I were to schedule a big conference called "Signs and Wonders" I would get a huge turnout. But if I held a big convention and I called it "Crucifixion of the Flesh" nobody would want to come. If I advertised it and said, "Come, we're going to pray—we're going to fast. The café will be closed tonight," nobody would want to come. But if I said, "Signs and Wonders, free pizza and drinks," it would be packed out. Why? Because everybody likes to do what's easy. These days it's not popular to preach and write these things because our flesh rebels at the idea of obeying the Master's voice. Please track with me for a bit, let's explore this great war within.

I want to be your Queen. I want to be ready for my King of Kings! I die to my own desires that I may live for you alone. I yield that I may follow hard after you! I am your submitted Bride and you are the Lover of my Soul!

CHAPTER 16

The War Within

In this life you're going to have to go through a battle and it won't be an easy one, but God promises us in Exodus 14:14, **"God will fight my battle and I will hold my peace."** He will help you, His grace will be sufficient for you if you are willing to yield to the Spirit, but He is not going to jump in your body and make you conform into the very image of Christ, He is not going to force you die to self, He is not going to crucify your flesh if you are unwilling. You have to be willing to say, "Holy Spirit, even if it causes me pain and I must crucify this flesh, I'm going to yield to the Spirit because I'm going to do what's right no matter what!"

The wonderful news is that if you want to be counted with the mature Bride of Jesus Christ described in Revelation 19 you must crucify your flesh, denying yourself. You'll then have to pick up your cross and follow after God, and sometimes you're not going to feel like it. You're not going to feel like praying or submitting to God; you're not going to feel like fasting, you're not going to feel like seeking, you're not going feel like knocking or pressing in. Sometimes you're going to feel like coasting, you're going to feel like you can't fight another minute, like setting aside your armor and sword to curl up for a little nap, but that's when you say, "Forget it, Satan! That's not going to happen! Not today! Not ever!"

Let me ask you a question: Are you going to follow after ex-Queen Vashti? Are you going to give in to the temptation to rebel, refusing to be told what to do? Are you going that direction in opposition to the will of God? There's no way we should want to do that.

In Esther Chapter 2 verses 1-4, it says, **"But after a serious anger subsided, he began thinking about Vashti and what she had done and the decree that he had made, so his personal attendants suggested, 'Let us search the empire to find a beautiful young virgin for the king. Let the king appoint agents in each province to bring these beautiful young women into the royal harem at the fortress of Susa, and the kings eunuch in charge of the harem will see that she be given all the beauty treatments; after that the young women who most pleases the king will be made queen instead of Vashti.' This advice was very appealing to the king so he put out the plan into effect."**

So here we see the king rejecting the rebellious Vashti and seeking to replace her with a new queen. The same thing is happening today in the church. God is seeking after His queen—a mature Bride who has a heart for her Groom. And just as the king became upset and rejected the rebellious nature of His queen, God is also rejecting the flesh in these end times; He will accept nothing but a wise virgin for His Bride.

Soaking, Saturating in the Ointment of the Holy Spirit

Look at verse 12: **"Before each young woman was taken to the king's chambers, she was given the prescribed twelve months of beauty treatments, six months with oil of myrrh, followed by six months with special perfumes and ointments. When it was time for her to go to the king's palace she was given her choice of whatever clothing or jewelry she wanted to take from the harem. That evening she was taken to the king's private rooms and the next morning she was brought to the second harem where the king's wives lived."**

Look closely at the process this beautiful bride Esther goes through: a year-long purification process, preparing her for one night with the king. In other words, she didn't go strolling into his chambers and say, "Hey, I'm Esther." In fact, she went through months of preparation: she had to soak in certain types of ointments and perfumes and fragrances. She had to be as attractive as possible to vie with other contestants for the attention of a king, to save her nation from extinction.

Did you know that there is also a **purification process** through which the Lord takes His Bride, where she's soaking, saturating herself in the ointment of the Holy Spirit? She is purifying, preparing to be that mature Bride He is seeking, the one she will love and serve with all her heart, forever. Let's dig deeper into this. Read on...

Give me the grace, my Lord, to battle any desire of the flesh that I may be prepared for the chambers of the King. Purify me! Burn up the carnality of my flesh that I may be your golden Queen of the Spirit!

CHAPTER 17

Purification of the Bride

There is a purification that is coming to the church. In May of 1993, I was right out of Bible school when I had my first vision. I was downstairs in the family room sitting on a hope chest when I saw a powerful wind blow through a church and a broom begin to sweep from the back of the church all the way up to the pulpit. I was amazed at what I'd seen. My heart pounded hard in my chest as I saw the windows blow open and the wind blowing through the church when the Lord said, "I'm cleansing my temple. I'm purifying my people and I'm causing the wind of the Holy Spirit to blow from the back row to the pulpit to purify it completely."

Since that day I've held on to that word knowing that God is doing exactly that—purifying His Bride in preparation for His soon return. The cleansing of both our hearts and the corporate body of the church.

Why Is It so Challenging?

Sometimes it's challenging to really be sold out to God; it's sacrificing to really run after the Lord with all our heart. It will cost you something to really chase after the things of God because there is purification and a requirement—a price that many aren't willing to pay. More often than not, people want easy street religion. And sometimes it seems that He's requiring things that are tough and that seem strange and hard to understand. In fact, you may ask yourself, *Man, why in the world would He require such a thing? It just doesn't make sense to me. Why is it so challenging?* We live in a day where people expect things for free, so it's not surprising that we want a worldwide ministry without paying a price. We want the benefits of the cross without dying daily. We want the beauty and blessings of the Lord but without crucifying the flesh. We want it all, but we want it free or for little cost.

We hate to hear about fasting. It's just too hard. I can remember many times years ago when, after church, someone would come up to me and say, "Hey Steve, the Lord told me that I was to take you out to eat."

And I would smile and say, "Oh, thank you. That would be great."

Then I followed them to the restaurant where I sat in my car, only to hear the Lord say, "Cancel the meal and fast."

The first thing that I wanted to do was say, "Get thee behind me, Satan. You're trying to rob me of a good meal!" But the plain truth is that sometimes the Lord wanted to test my obedience.

Is my obedience nothing but empty words or does it require action on my part? Am I speaking merely hollow words that don't match up with my life message or my preaching? Are they just emotional expressions that I forget as soon as I get away from church for a day or two? There were times when I was disobedient and refused to listen and later carried the regret for days. And many times I had to go to my host and say, "I'm sorry but the Lord has called me to fast and pray." It always feels awkward when I have to do things like that.

You presume that people think, *He thinks he's so spiritual.* I certainly don't want to come across as holier than thou, so I rarely ever use the word "fasting". I've often tried to make some reasonable excuse but it always sounded lame, and I could see the look of disappointment on their faces. That sometimes makes it hard to be obedient to the Lord.

The Testing

I remember once, when our children were small, my wife Diane said, "Let's take the kids to the carnival."

I was all excited about going when I said, "Kids, we're going to go to the carnival. I'm going to buy tickets so you can go on all the great rides. We'll get cotton candy and eat caramel apples." When I told them, their faces lit up with excitement and we hurried to get ready. As we were getting in the car the Lord said, "Don't go. Pray." At that particular time, I'd been crying out to God, saying things like, "No matter how hard it is, Lord, I'll do what you say. I surrender all!"

Thankfully, my precious wife, Diane, understood, but the looks on my kids' faces really crushed me because they didn't understand. "What do you mean Jesus told you that we can't have candy apples?"

"Oh, there goes dad, being spiritual again."

Who knows what they were thinking, but it was clear that they were terribly disappointed.

I went upstairs, closed the door, knelt by my bed and began to weep because I felt like I had really let them down. I said, "Holy Spirit, here I am. Whatever you want to say to me, whatever you want to do, I'm here."

And this is what the Holy Spirit said: "You've passed the test. Now go take your kids to the carnival and have a good time." He just wanted to see **if I was willing** to be obedient, much like the story of Abraham and Isaac.

I recall when I was on staff in a particularly lukewarm church. It was really tough—the hardest two years of my life. I used to sit on the front pew and that lukewarm spirit was so strong it would choke me every service. I would go into my office and cry, grieving over the cold barrenness there. One Sunday, after service, I was talking to Diane about my pastor, and in his absence I just let him have it. But I knew I wasn't saying it in the right spirit; I had a check about it even as I was speaking.

I didn't say a thing to anyone else; I only shared it with my wife. But a couple of days later, we were in a staff meeting with other pastors. The one I spoke against had his doctorate degree and he was very analytical—the most intelligent pastor I'd ever met in my life, like a Jack Hayford. He knew his Bible better than anyone I've ever seen; he knew Greek, and Hebrew; he would scrutinize every word people said and analyze the meaning behind it. He truly was brilliant.

During the meeting my heart was beating loud and hard, and in front of the whole room the Holy Spirit said, "Repent, Steve."

I silently responded, "I'm not going to do that. There is no way!" But have you noticed that the voice of the Holy Spirit only grows louder when you try to ignore it? You swear everyone in that building can hear your heart beating: baboom, baboom baboom.

And all of a sudden I said, "Pastor, I have something I have to say. I want to ask you to forgive me," and I began to cry. "Forgive me. I said things about you in the wrong spirit." And then the dam opened, and another pastor also asked forgiveness, then another, until the room was silent. I had never seen anything like that before or since, regarding a repentance revival among the staff. Everyone was weeping and repenting of things.

Once it was over the Lord said to me, "Steve, because you humbled yourself, I will now lift you up." And it wasn't long after that that He moved me out of there, into a place where I was able to preach what was on my heart, and He moved in power. From that point on, I was celebrated rather than tolerated wherever I went.

I can't tell you how hard it was to say, "Pastor," because I knew he was going to analyze me. He was going to study my face, and at first he did. "I have a confession to make . . ."

I knew he was thinking, *Oh, Steve is going to confess! I know the definition of the Greek word confession, it means...* He was a nice man, he really was. I love and admire him, and I wish him the best, but it was tough working with him and eating humble pie was even harder.

I Had to Learn to Submit Myself Under Authority

Who says it's easy to become the mature Bride of Jesus Christ? Who says it's easy to crucify your flesh? Who says it's easy to pick up your cross, deny yourself and follow after God? But if you want to be that mature Bride of Jesus Christ, it's going to cost you everything. Truthfully, you're going to have to repeatedly eat humble pie, but you'll never be lifted up until you learn to humble yourself and be obedient to God. I've learned this the hard way many times.

Before the Lord ever gave me a ministry that was dear to my heart, I had to learn to submit myself under authority, and it wasn't always easy. Some of the pastors that I served . . . well, the truth is that, while some were wonderful, some were very difficult.

The Lord would tell me, "You submit under that authority," and it was tough; it was hard to go to different ones and repent, but the reality is it's never easy to deny our flesh. But if we go through the purification process, obeying what God says, we'll be in line to carry the very presence of God in a special way. On the other hand, you'll never be a carrier of the presence if you have an arrogant, unteachable spirit. It's a spirit of meekness that attracts the presence of God.

Until you learn to humble yourself, you will never be a true carrier of the powerful presence of God. To humble yourself you need to say, "Father, even if it kills me, I'm going to humble myself, I'm going to be obedient. I'm going to do Your will. I know it won't be easy, Lord, but I'm going to do it if you'll help me."

Then Father says, "You know what? I'm going to saturate you with my presence because I'm attracted to your meekness. I love those that lean upon me."

The Lord once said to me, **"If Saul is trying to kill you, are you being a David?"** David never asked for a Saul in his life—it wasn't fair. I mean David was running from the king, who wanted to kill him, even threw spears at him. Yet even when he had the chance, he humbled himself and never once touched God's anointed—King Saul. In the end, David became one of the greatest kings Israel ever had because he humbled himself; the same is true of us; when we learn to humble ourselves, God will lift us up.

The Bride must go through a purification process, and if we want to be a mature Bride, we're not going to go around announcing it or wear a sticker that says, "I'm a big deal; I am the Bride!" There should be no Bride pride but only a meek and humble spirit that has been processed by the Lord. We are going to have to go through purification, and in the process, you may be chased by a couple of Sauls. You may have to give up some things. You may have to deny yourself. But you must be willing to be obedient so that you can eat the good of the land. (See Isaiah 1:19)

That I may be humble in your sight. That I may know you...really know you. May the beauty of the Lord be upon me, that when others see me... they see you! Even if a Saul is after me I turn to you ... for in you is everything I need. Transform me, my Lord. This is what I am after!

CHAPTER 18

The Favor of God That Rests

So what happens when you go through the purification process? Let's look at Chapter 2 of Esther verse 16, where it says, **"Esther was taken to the King Ahasuerus at the royal palace in early winter of the seventh year of his reign. And the King loved Esther more than any of the other young women; he was so delighted with her that he set the royal crown on her head and declared her Queen to replace Vashti. To celebrate the occasion, he threw a great banquet for all his nobles and officials in Esther's honor, declaring a public holiday in the provinces and giving generous gifts to everyone."** (v.17)

So here we see Esther, who is prepared after bathing and soaking in oils, doing what she knew she needed to do. And because of her obedience, the favor of God rested upon her. Today I declare that if you are preparing yourself to be the mature Bride of Jesus Christ, you'll have God's favor and anointing resting upon you so that you'll be blessed in every step you take.

The favor of God (His approbation) will rest upon you as you draw near and prepare yourself, submitting to Him in every area of your life. If we want the favor of God we must be willing to prepare ourselves, to purify, to pick up our cross and follow hard after Him. We must be willing to do the hard things like eating humble pie. When we make mistakes, we must be willing to admit them and make things right. When we offend others, we need to ask forgiveness and reconcile with each other.

"Those who belong to Christ Jesus have <u>crucified the flesh</u> with its passions and desires" Galatians 5:24 (NLT).

As I said before it's not easy. But who said it would be? Let's take a look at this word "crucify" again. Notice how Paul uses the phrase, "Crucify the flesh." Literal crucifixion means massive nails pounded through your hands and feet, which is excruciating, but in the same way the crucifixion of your flesh is the prerequisite for becoming a mature Bride, where His divine favor rests upon you.

The Shulamite in the Song of Solomon went through purification to be a carrier of the very manifest presence of God by opening the door to the knocks and yearnings of the heart of her bridegroom.

As we end this section I want you to ponder the Lord's call to come. Will you respond to the call with a yes answer, soaking in His presence in order to be a carrier of the very glory of God? I've seen two kinds of responses to the call of God. One of them says, "What am I going to wear?" She isn't prepared because she isn't willing to pay the price to get to know Him. Finally, the wedding day arrives, and she asks herself, *What on earth am I doing? What am I getting myself into?*

Then there's the mature Bride who knows and is intimately acquainted with the Lord, and because she trusts Him implicitly, she's willing to submit her life to His leadership. She has yielded to the voice of the Holy Spirit, and because she refuses to harden her heart, she's a carrier of the presence. Father is looking for those who will yield so they can carry the presence. Let's dare to be carriers!

Make me a carrier of your presence! I will not harden my heart ... make me soft and pliable that your presence would wrap around me. I submit under your leadership as I am conformed into your same image! I trust you so have your way in me!

CHAPTER 19

The Shepherd's Tent

"**Tell me, O thou whom my soul loveth, where thou feedest, where thou makest thy flock to rest at noon: for why should I be as one that turneth aside by the flocks of thy companions? If thou know not, O thou fairest among women, go thy way forth by the footsteps of the flock, and feed thy kids beside the shepherds' tents**" (Song of Solomon 1:7-8).

I often revisit the same vision when I pray. I see a long path leading far into the distance. The sun is just setting on the horizon. Lanterns light both sides of the path guiding the traveler toward his goal. These lanterns were carefully positioned by pioneers from ages gone by, each lantern illuminating the way for the spiritually sensitive travelers who seek the secrets of the well-lit path.

The Bridegroom places a deep desire within His Bride to spend time with Him, to be His confidante. The testimony of others encourages her to keep going, but she doesn't want to stop there. She must forge ahead herself, crying out with intense spiritual hunger, **"Tell me more..."** She needs more than just the overflow of someone else's experience; *"The flock of thy companions"* is no longer enough. She needs more than just the testimony or ministry of someone else, which cannot address her deepest need for His presence. She begins a diligent search for others who really know Him personally, those few who understand *His ways—not just His acts.*

She must follow the *"footsteps of the flock"* taking the road less traveled to learn their secrets and follow their example on the way to the *"Shepherd's tent."* It's there that she, too, will be captivated by His love and favor. It's at the *Shepherd's tent* that she learns truths she can only learn for herself by getting to know the personal Bridegroom who embraces her in a deeply personal way.

There the *pioneer* is transformed into the *light bearer,* and the journey now becomes a testimony borne of personal intimacy. Others receive hope as they follow the *"footsteps of the flock."* The path is illuminated by the precious truth of their testimony, which soon becomes a guiding light, a beacon lighting the way for others who clearly sense God's approval on them as His fragrance flows from inside them.

Pioneers of the faith placed the lanterns on that long path I saw in my vision. The lanterns represent the *"footsteps of the flock"* on the path before us, placed by pioneers like Wade Taylor, Walter Beuttler, Brother Lawrence, Hattie Hammond, Father Nash, and Praying Hyde. They each left a lantern, a landmark testimony, so we may more clearly see the path ahead. We have hope that we too may reach the *"Shepherds tent,"* to know Him and receive a personal revelation from the One who loves us most.

As other pioneers of the past have blazed a trail led by your presence, let me also blaze a trail and leave a legacy for others who come behind me!

CHAPTER 20

The Lantern Left by Wade Taylor

Wade Taylor was my spiritual father for over twenty-three years. Wade had something remarkable—a unique walk with his God that enabled him to carry the manifest presence of the Lord. His deeper walk encouraged us to pursue God for ourselves, to also obtain the abiding manifest presence of God in our lives.

I vividly remember those nights with Brother Taylor at Pinecrest Bible Training Center in Salisbury Center, NY as the flames of fire were fanned in my life. I remember lying on my face in my dorm for hours, basking in the glory of the Lord. I was transformed by the manifest presence of God. A fire for the deeper things of the Spirit still burns within me, sparked by those times spent with him in prayer.

I'll always be grateful to Brother Taylor. I love him very much. He was never too "big" or busy to invest in my life. Words cannot express how much I miss him since his graduation to Heaven. He was a true spiritual father, always just a phone call away; his prayers and loving commitment were powerful. It brings me to tears every time I think about the difference he made in my life over the years I knew him. I will see him again in eternity.

I still remember the last time I saw him before his passing on February 29 of 2012. We had spoken at a conference together in upstate NY. We made the long drive together and had a truly meaningful conversation during our trip. When we arrived back at his home in Washington, DC, we prayed together, and he once again prayed impartation and treasured truths into me, and then we took communion. He accompanied me when I took the train to the airport. At the airport he told me how much our time had meant to him and invited me to visit him again. He stood there as I went through the gate to catch my plane. His humility and the presence he carried affected me even as we said our goodbyes. I was deeply blessed during the trip. What an honor to have a friend like Wade Taylor.

The Beginning

Wade Taylor has authored four devotional books, which have touched countless lives around the world, *The Secret of the Stairs, Waterspouts of Glory, Unlocking the Mysteries of the Kingdom,* and *Being Made Ready – A Daily Devotional.*

His walk with the Lord began in the mid-1950s when the Lord called him to sell two successful businesses—a general insurance agency and a cable television company—in order to more fully concentrate on preparation for the Lord's calling on his life.

In the fall of 1956, Wade enrolled as a student at the Eastern Bible Institute (EBI) in Green Lane, Pennsylvania where one of his teachers, Walter Beuttler, had a profound influence on his life. Beuttler encouraged his students to cultivate a personal and experiential knowledge of the Lord.

Through the example of Walter Beuttler's personal walk with the Lord, and the "impartation" of his teachings into Wade Taylor's life, two transforming qualities were established:

The value of spending quality time "Waiting on the Lord" and seeking to cultivate a hearing ear to better hear the voice of the Lord and respond to His presence.

After graduating from the Eastern Bible Institute, Wade purposed to start a church in the city of Philadelphia, but the Lord had different plans. For the next 35 years, he was involved in ministry in two different Bible schools.

In 1998, due to having received a very specific word from the Lord to relocate to the Nation's capital, Wade moved to Washington, DC. He had an on-going burden for the establishing of the Kingdom of God.

The much-coveted qualities of spiritual excellence, which have been the defining attributes of his life and ministry, are now being imparted to the Body of Christ at large through his website, www.wadetaylor.org, and these four books he has published, which are available on his publications website, www.wadetaylorpublications.org. [1]

"Downloaded" with Spirit and Life

Wade loved to tell a powerful story that I want to share with you. While waiting upon the Lord, he'd been caught up and completely engulfed in the visible glory that he saw in brilliant color as he stood before the throne of God. He shared how a rainbow's light went through him. When the Lord brought him back to the here and now, he could not function for some time. At that time, he didn't have the words to describe what had happened, but later he described how he was "downloaded" with spirit and life as well as understanding that he didn't previously possess.

It was very evident from Wade's ministry that day that God had especially anointed his words to communicate the deeper truths of the Word, a unique word to prepare the Bride for the soon return of the Lord in His kingdom.

In 1957, Wade received a very special revelation of the Song of Solomon. The Lord allowed him to experience the progression of events within the Song of Solomon from the perspective of each of the participants, feeling as they felt and thinking their thoughts.

This profound experience lasted several hours. When the Spirit of the Lord lifted, Wade realized that a deeper understanding of the Song of Solomon, from a new and fresh perspective, had been imparted to him. [2]

Our Brother Taylor was a gifted and anointed teacher who taught primarily by prophetic revelation and impartation. He was most at home in the classroom, where for thirty-five years he faithfully taught those truths and divine principles. He offered them to those who had ears to hear! One of his favorite reference points was: **"If ye be willing and obedient, ye shall eat the good of the land"** (Isaiah 1:19).

Thank God for the great number who welcomed such truths with ears to hear and hearts to understand—who heard the call to: "Come-up, higher," and by our Lord's grace, unto their response, they were lifted up into the greatness of God. [3]"

Within the life of Wade Taylor we see a hunger for the Bridegroom. I've been in prayer with him as he cried out, "Draw me!" That intense spiritual desire has stirred a hunger and left a lantern for many of his spiritual children throughout the years. May this great man of God holding a bright lantern inspire you also to seek God with tremendous hunger! Start today!

Steve Porter

"Words cannot express how much I miss you. Wade, you were a true spiritual father; you were always just a phone call away, your prayers were powerful, and your love always felt. It brings me to tears every time I think about the difference you made in my life over the 20 + years I knew you. I will see you again in eternity. I promise to make you proud as I run my race."

— *Steve*

1. Parousia Ministries: www.wadetaylor.org

2. Book: *The Secret of the Stairs* by Wade Taylor

3. A Tribute to Wade and Mae Taylor - Michael O'Connor

CHAPTER 21

My Company of Overcomers

"And they have defeated him by the blood of the Lamb and by their testimony. And they did not love their lives so much that they were afraid to die" (Revelation 12:11).

"Little children, you are from God and have overcome them, for he who is in you is greater than he who is in the world" (1 John 4:4).

In prayer, I recently saw a vast army of men and women, standing, looking regal and confident, awaiting marching orders. Yet they appeared more like kings, queens and priests than I anticipated. Their nobility was a badge of honor. Their faces shined brightly, reflecting the very glory of God, filled with yearning as their hearts burned with a passion for more of Him. Their countenance literally caused me to shudder and shake because they carried the authority of Heaven. Every word they spoke was anointed and carried a holy presence that could not be denied.

This army stood on a battlefield but without a single iota of fear in their demeanor. Among them were men, women and children—people from every nation and tongue—standing shoulder to shoulder, connected by brotherly love, dignity, and honor and passion for Christ.

Then the Lord said, **"They were the ones who once lay wounded, victims of warfare, but I lifted them up, restored them and empowered them to be My Overcomers. They are a part of my end time Bride who shall advance My kingdom purposes on Earth."**

All at once, Satan came at them in a last-ditch effort to drive these dear ones into the valley of defeat, *but* the Lord would not allow it. He quickly came to rescue them as they stood strong in faith and in the power of His might.

I sensed the Lord saying, "Satan has tried to destroy them, trying to convince them that they are not delivered, restored and healed. He's assaulted them with negative missiles to tear them down in defeat."

Then I saw pictures of face after face of those who sought to injure and destroy this vast and beloved army. Satan thought he was sneaky and whispered lies into their ears, saying, "Remember that one who wounded you and left you to die? Remember that betrayal and that other past wound that was festering—how can you forgive that?"

All at once, the vast army chose to stand their ground, applying the blood of Christ and the power of forgiveness to their hearts and minds, so that Satan was once again soundly defeated and fled in terror. I could hear the deafening sound of God's army chanting, "Victory is ours! Victory is ours through the shed blood of the Lamb. Victory is ours!" Their declarations filled the air with a sound of Heaven when they refused to allow the enemy's victim mentality to take root. Instead, they offered up the most anointed praise to God. This praise was the weapon that caused Satan to lose that battle. The victory chant led to a mighty explosion of glorious praise and worship!

The Lord is saying, **"Stand your ground! Do not allow the enemy even an instant of thought."** When he comes to assault you with flaming missiles of past hurt and blame, the Lord wants you to hear this: "I will win the war for the battle is Mine. I will infuse you with My power, and you shall stand strong and be My company of Overcomers. For even the devastating wounds that you once experienced that could have destroyed you are healed by My righteous right hand!" Today, the Lord says, "YOU will not lose ground if you PRAISE your way to victory, letting go of past hurts and wounds by the power of forgiveness, and stand strong as My company of Overcomers! I have called you to OVERCOME! Victory is yours, so grab hold of it with everything in you and march on!"

The Heavenly Bridegroom Will Have an Overcoming Bride!

"If we endure, we will also reign with him. If we disown him, he will also disown us;" (2 Timothy 2:12).

Every day we have opportunities to choose to overcome the obstacles in our paths or to become apathetic. We can choose to walk a deeper, more consecrated life or we can choose to surrender to a lukewarm and faint-hearted spirit. If we endure and choose obedience we will then reign with Christ in His kingdom. Even as Adam and Eve had the power to choose, so do we, in this life.

"To him that overcometh will I grant to sit with me in my throne, even as I also overcame, and am set down with my Father in his throne" (Revelation 3:21).

We are to be the "overcoming" Bride who will rise above life's temporary disruptions and yield our lives to the Lord. These "Overcomers" will rule and reign with Christ and be given spiritual authority because they have learned in this life to come under His authority. The Heavenly Bridegroom will have a submitted Bride that leans on Him alone.

"To the one who overcomes and does my will to the end, I will give authority over the nations" (Revelation 2:26).

May we all hear those cherished words from the Father as we stand before Him—**"Well done thou good and faithful servant"** (Matthew 25:21)—because we made the right choices here on Earth.

Be Ready

Our Heavenly Bridegroom is looking for a Bride willing to be transformed into a "vessel of honor" fit for His use. This transformation takes place in the lives of believers who are proactively submitting to the process of God. This process includes actions or changes that prepare people for the work God has called them to do. This process, as I said, is never an easy one, but rather it is the "molding" and "shaping" through our obedience that transforms us into vessels that bring honor. We are His workmanship. Let's look at this key scripture one more time.

Revelation 19:7-9 (KJV): **"Let us be glad and rejoice, and give honor to him: for the marriage of the Lamb is come, and <u>his wife hath made herself ready</u>. And to her was granted that she should be arrayed in fine linen, clean and white: <u>for the fine linen is the righteousness of saints</u>. And he saith unto me, Write, Blessed are they which <u>are called</u> unto the marriage supper of the Lamb. And he saith unto me, these are the true sayings of God."**

We see in this text that the Lord's desire is to find a mature Bride who has done what is necessary to make herself ready for Him, one who, by her own free will, has arrayed herself in the prescribed wedding garments. She is not forced, but having been given a choice, she makes that choice out of reckless abandon for her beloved.

Just like I shared the Esther story previously we also live in that age of preparation and equipping. Father is now offering us an opportunity to prepare for eternity in His kingdom, but it's our choice whether or not we will prepare. We may wonder if preparation is even possible, and, if so, what that process encompasses. **Adequate preparation is only possible with the help of the Holy Spirit**; the training is not easy and requires effort on the part of each individual. Spiritual maturity does not come through a prayer line and is not imparted but is walked out in every person's life.

Maturity Is a Process

Hebrews 12:29 says, **"For our God is a consuming fire."** He purges us through the fire. A heart purged with fire is a heart consumed by His love. His divine nature is fashioned in us as the impurities surface. When we deal with these impurities, we grow to be like Jesus as His mature Bride.

The process of arrow-making takes great patience. High quality, dependable arrows cannot be made in haste. Skilled Old Testament archers actually began making their arrows one year in advance. They first had to find just the right kind of wood, most often the branches of an almond tree because its branches grew straighter than any other and it was one of the first to bud in spring. For our purposes, the almond tree symbolizes **"resurrection power"**. Father uses great patience to develop us into vessels of honor. As the fire burns away the dross (sin) in our lives, our obedience produces resurrection power (the budding of the almond tree) that burns away the old things, and we become brand new creatures in Christ.

Once the branch was cut down the next step was to strip off the bark. Dead bark represents the removal of the flesh. Maturity takes time. Once He cuts the knots (strongholds) and burrs (bad habits) from our lives we become the type of arrow God can use. "Stripping" is never comfortable but is a part of the process. Joseph was stripped of his coat of many colors (favor) before he finally put on the garments of a ruler. He endured a painful stripping process before he eventually became the prime minister (polished arrow) of a powerful nation.

Just as anxiety is mounting in the Earth today, a beautiful Bride is being prepared like that arrow. The "beauty of the Lord" is upon her; her face is bright, glistening with the light of the glory of God. Her train is long, shimmering with brilliant rays of light. Her countenance is difficult to gaze upon as the dazzling atmosphere of heaven surrounds her. Abba Father is busy preparing a Bride for His Son. The Bride is "buying gold tried by fire"—His divine nature.

In any dark days ahead, we must allow the "fire" to burn away our sin and conform us into the image of His Son. His nature changes our nature so that others will say, **"Who is this that comes out of the wilderness, leaning on her lover?"** (Song of Solomon 8:5) His Bride will be an end-time witness and she will be that sign and wonder to all the Earth. She will be as a city set on a hill that cannot be hidden and others will see her good works and glorify the Father. (Matthew 5:14, 16) She will be named amongst that overcoming remnant because she has learned to endure; therefore she will also reign with Him!

Lord, teach me to obey, to yield to the Spirit in all things, and to do your will to the very end that I may invest in the life to come as Your Overcoming Bride.

CHAPTER 22

The Upward Call

O my dove, that art in the clefts of the rock, in the <u>secret</u> *places* <u>of the stairs</u>, let me see thy countenance, let me hear thy voice; for sweet is thy voice, and thy countenance is comely"
(Song of Solomon 2:14, KJV).

Let's continue our journey toward our Heavenly Bridegroom into His "chambers"—His dwelling place. The Lord offers intimate communion and a deeper love relationship with Him. Repetition is the best teacher so let's review what we've learned so far:

My beloved spake, and said unto me, Rise up, my love, my fair one, and come away (Song of Solomon 2:10).

He calls to His Bride to "Rise up" and prepares stairs for those who hunger to climb higher into His presence. Our quest for intimacy can begin today as we seek the satisfaction we long for and for which we were created.

He stands bidding us to be partakers of His holy presence—calling those who want to move past the holy place through the veil into the "Holy of Holies".

He's calling us upward toward personal intimacy and into a new realm of glory. Each step in the staircase represents a new level of intimacy obtained. It should be our deepest desire to keep climbing higher each day as we yearn for deeper communion with the Lord that will lead to increasing spiritual growth. No matter what dark night we face or what obstacle we must overcome, we climb higher each day as we keep our focus on Him.

A deep longing is being birthed in the heart of His Bride for divine encounters of the God kind. Not just a self-serving desire for only His blessings and manifestations, but an earnest seeking of His face alone. He is placing in us an intense spiritual hunger and desire for Him as He reveals the secret entrance to the stairway. It's there we can meet with Him alone. His Bride will not stop until she has connected with His heart. These stairs contain greater levels of communion. With each step the level of intimacy increases. The thing is that when we travel upward, there's no turning back. We are transformed forever by His fervent love.

The Invisible Church

We're indeed living in the end times and we all know it will get tougher before the Lord comes and reigns on this Earth and uproots all evil. I can't wait until we fully transition into the kingdom age! We are currently living in times like Noah.

But the Lord is busy preparing a Bride and she is making herself ready. Father will have a church within the church—a people within a people, His remnant. Many in the church are in a backslidden state—they've been engulfed in the "great falling away" through their "itching ears" and disobedience. They've embraced a feel-good gospel, a true Babylonian word, and slowly the spirit of Laodicea has choked the presence from their lives. Now all that's left is form and dead religion without Spirit and Life.

This has brought about an embracing of the world's system—whatever is cool, trendy, and politically correct. BUT do not be dismayed. The Heavenly Bridegroom is wooing those from the greater church who will stand firm and become a church within the church—an invisible church known only to God. The wise virgins of Matthew 25 are busy keeping oil in their lamps because the Bridegroom is standing at the door and knocking.

"Behold, I stand at the door, and knock: if any man hears my voice, and opens the door, I will come in to him, and will eat with him, and he with me" (Revelation 3:20).

Our Heavenly Bridegroom desires to come inside. In this verse we see Him standing at the door yearning to enter and commune with us. The "door" in this verse speaks to the heart of the lukewarm Christian.

"So then because you are lukewarm, and neither cold nor hot, I will spew you out of My mouth. Because you say, I am rich, and increased with goods, and have need of nothing; and know not that you are wretched, and miserable, and poor, and blind, and naked" (Revelation 3:16-17).

Again, consider the parable of the ten virgins in light of the message of the Bride.

The foolish virgins took no oil with them, while the wise ones had filled their vessels with oil. They were ready. (Matthew 25:3-4). If there is to be room for oil in our vessels, they must first be emptied of the things that don't matter. We must make room for the Lord to enter and dwell!

He Prepares a Table

May I remind you one last time that the Lord has prepared a feasting table for those that are hungry for more of Him? He stands bidding us to be partakers in His holy presence. He is calling those that want to move past the holy place through the veil into the Holy of Holies. As I said before a deep longing is being birthed in the heart of His Bride for divine encounters of the God kind, not seeking His hands but His face. He is opening portals of His glory for us to encounter. His Bride will not stop until she has experienced His majesty. These portals contain the atmosphere of Heaven; they're a direct link between Heaven and Earth. Can we experience the same atmosphere as the one in the throne room? How could we not?

Does Father desire for His manifest presence to invade this Earth? Yes! God is pouring out His Spirit upon the spiritually thirsty and the spiritually discontent. He's creating portals from the throne above the lives of His Bride and places that seek Him with all their hearts. Many are already walking in this realm. There are deeper dimensions in Abba Father (John 14:2) that we haven't yet entered. Places in the spirit we haven't seen. These portals of His glory are pouring out on those that desire the deeper realms of the spirit. A direct connection to the atmosphere of Heaven is being granted to a Bride who has fully submitted to loving Him. She is answering His knocks and resting with Him in daily communion.

"I love them that Love me. Those that search for me will surely find me" (Proverbs 8:17).

Divine mysteries are being revealed to His Bride. Kingdom revelation is being imparted in the lives of those that hunger for the deeper realms of God. Abba's secrets are being whispered in the inner ears of His cherished ones—those that wait for a portal to open in their secret place with Him.

"But we know these things because God has revealed them to us by his Spirit, and his Spirit searches out everything and shows us even God's deep secrets" (1 Corinthians 2:10).

We're living in the times and seasons when Father will begin to pour out His Spirit on all flesh. A divine door will open and His glory will fall upon His Bride once again. The moving of His Spirit will refresh her. The Bride will have her revival. Huge gatherings of hungry lovers of God will experience a portal of glory being opened over their meetings. Signs and wonders, healings, miracles, and deliverances will take place as a deluge of His Spirit is released. How can anything stand against it when His majesty is revealed? When God opens His spout where the glory comes out, sickness will bow the knee to the King of Kings. God will even do a fresh new thing. Some will misunderstand while others will embrace the new thing.

In the end times, entire gatherings will be healed. I see creative miracles happening as the light of His glory invades a place through a portal. Demons will tremble as the true church is infused with the flames of His Spirit. Children will manifest creative arts and be entrusted with secrets from the throne room. That which has been shut up in the heavens will finally be released.

Divine secret truth will even be unsealed and released as the atmosphere of Heaven freely flows. Now is the time; the hour is late, so we must prepare for the kingdom age and get ready for deeper dimensions in Abba. Now is the season! The portals of glory are opening on a Bride who seeks first His kingdom and leans upon His breast to hear the heartbeat of the Bridegroom as lover and friend.

Let His Kingdom Come!

Our Heavenly Bridegroom wants nothing more than for you to draw near to Him to accomplish the *"end-time"* kingdom purposes for which He has drawn you to Himself. Now is the time! Prepare and make yourself ready!

Right now He's equipping that body of "overcomers" made ready through preparation. Much like a bride prepares for her wedding day, His Bride will be prepared and ready, her lamp filled with oil, her life set apart to do His will. She is made ready and can testify that our Lord has *"made us ... kings and priests,"* and as a result will have an active part with Him in the outworking of His end-time purposes to establish His Kingdom.

"Thy kingdom come. Thy will be done in earth, as it is in heaven"

(Matthew 6:10).

As His kingdom comes, chains are broken, lives are set free by His power, and people are delivered from bondage. When His kingdom comes, mountains have to move; the Earth shakes with the very manifest glory of God and every tongue declares that He is Lord. When His kingdom comes everything changes, creative power is released, darkness is defeated, and His Bride will take her rightful place where she will rule and reign with Him as His glory is made manifest through her. Others will take notice that she has been with Him because she is beautiful and reflects His glory—His delight.

Today He stands at the door of your heart, knocking, eager for you to enter that intimate relationship with Him as His stunningly beautiful, mature Bride. He is not coming for an immature bride but rather for a Bride prepared through her righteous acts. A right response when He knocks will lead you into an active, personal relationship with Him that will result in you having *a part* in the establishing of, and functioning in, His Kingdom. This requires of you a fixed upward gaze focused on Him, living a life surrendered to His will.

He's preparing a people in this day who are being *made ready* to function in this higher realm of spiritual authority, which will affect both the church and the nations. Therefore, it's imperative that you spend quality time "waiting" in the presence of the Lord with an upward gaze—that you might be able to hear and rightly respond to His call to function in His Kingdom as His mature Bride.

At this present time, Lord, there are those who are being called to "come up" into that higher level of relationship with You. I will answer the call, precious Lord, I will answer the call!

CHAPTER 23

The Bridegroom Takes Us by the Hands

Although some may struggle to believe what I am about to share, I can testify that it's true. I share this story with absolute integrity before the Lord.

In 2015, the Lord placed on my heart to fast and pray—to seek Him with all my heart—so I set aside a couple of weeks to seek Him afresh. I felt He had something to impart to me and I was seeking a fresh encounter. "Draw me" was my constant theme—a desire for more of Him.

I started my fast, and boy was it hard! The heavens were silent, and the Lord felt a hundred miles away. Sticking to my fast was quite the task, but my hunger for God compelled me to stay the course.

For two nights I had visitations from the enemy in my bedroom. The first night the enemy walked in and paralyzed me in my bed so that I couldn't move or even talk. I was completely frozen in place and felt defenseless. I was able to mutter the name, "Jesus!" and the enemy instantly fled. Oh, the power of the name of Jesus! At His name every demon must bow!

The second night, the enemy ramped it up a notch. With my physical eyes I saw a demon spirit swarm up at me and scream in my face. I cried out to Jesus to help me! And again Jesus came to the rescue and peace filled the room as I went back to sleep. I was safe in His presence. His angels had charge over the situation.

The following night, I went to sleep again. By now I had been fasting for over a week or so and I was weak and drained, not eager to confront any more demons. I went to sleep and was awakened suddenly by the presence of the Lord. A bright light filled the room, so bright that I couldn't see. I knew instinctively that Jesus had entered my room from the corner of the house. As He walked closer I heard the sound of bells ringing, and the sound of rushing wind blew through my room. He stood right in front of me and reached down and took one of my hands. He gently caressed my hand, and His divine love filled me. His power and majesty were so powerful that I couldn't move or even look at His face. All I could see was a bright light as the wind of God continued to blow. Suddenly, He was gone, and the vision ended.

I sat there amazed the Lord had come for me. As soon as I told Him how grateful I was, He instantly returned a second time. Again, I couldn't move as His power overwhelmed me and the rushing wind blew through my room. I felt His presence as I heard bells ringing and He slowly approached where I lay step by step. He stood in front of me and this time He took both of my hands. The Lord took my hands! He held my hands the same way Wade Taylor had often done, as if to impart something to me. After a few minutes, the Lord left the room and again I was back in the here and now.

I was overwhelmed by such a divine encounter. To think that Jesus cared enough about me to come and hold my hands and impart a gift to me! I felt unqualified and undeserving. Yet He had come. I had allowed my desperation for God over the past few years to cause me to pursue Him and He came to me. I heard the Lord say in my spirit, **"I will NOT be outdone by the enemy."** The enemy had come to pester me for two nights and the Lord would not be outdone. Therefore my Heavenly Bridegroom arrived, announcing His presence with bells, as my High Priest.

I have only shared this encounter publicly a few times because it was so special, so sacred. That Jesus would come to stand by me—that He would take my hands—it proved He cared enough to visit me.

As I close, I'm giving you a piece of my heart. I share the deep yearning of a Bride that is lovesick for her one and only. The one that is altogether lovely. He is bidding His Bride from amongst the daughters of Jerusalem to come away with Him and have deep, personal communion with Him.

As it now stands, the church can see her Bridegroom only by faith because she sees through a veil darkly, but it won't be long before a stunned world will hear the call, "Behold, the Bridegroom has arrived!" And a voice that sounds like loud thunder and the sound of many waters, will respond, **"Hallelujah, for the Lord God omnipotent reigns. Let us be glad, and rejoice, and give honor to Him, for the Marriage of the Lamb has come, and His wife has made herself ready"** (Revelation 19:7-9). Then He shall shine with a brightness none can abide, **"to be admired by His saints, and to be glorified by all those who believe"** (2 Thessalonians 1:10). His beautiful Bride shall be brought unto the King in clothing of incredibly fine tapestry; they will come with excited rejoicing and enter the King's quarters. The wedding song will be repeatedly sung: "Glory to the King of Kings and the Bridegroom!"

Guard Your Hearts from Distractions

With this book I am blowing the trumpet in Zion! Now it's time to prepare because it won't be long before He returns for us, those who have united ourselves to Him in love forever. So, until that day it's our responsibility to make sure that nothing hinders us from His presence. Nothing steals us from His embrace, nor will we willingly cease to sing His praise and obey what He tells us to do. So, guard your hearts from those who proclaim anything other than Jesus as King and Lord. Guard your hearts from distractions that would suck you in, saying there's another way to Heaven, for Jesus is the only way! We must continually examine our hearts to ensure that we hold no one and nothing dearer than Him. Cast down any golden idols and hold the line, stay the course, for He's coming soon!

You can feel it, can't you? Things are ramping up to a sudden, stunning climax of the ages. But many believers who were once hot for God no longer look with excitement for the return of our Savior. Rather, they've become distracted, idolatrous, lured to sleep by the enemy, believing that there will be no day of reckoning. In fact, many will stand at the gate of Heaven and say, "But Lord, didn't I do great things for you in Jesus' name? Didn't I cast out demons and heal the sick, even raising the dead on occasion? Don't you remember, Lord?"

And He will say these devastating words: **"Depart from Me. I never knew you!"** (See Matthew 7:22)

The thing is that it doesn't have to end that way. There's still time to repent and run, run, run back to our first love, and seek the Lord with all our hearts. There's still time to ask the Lord to renew a right spirit in us and draw us back to His chambers, fanning the flames of passion for Him alone. It's time to get serious about the things of the Lord, to seek His face, ask Him for our marching orders, and then tell everyone, far and wide that Jesus is coming soon! This close relationship between us and our Heavenly Bridegroom is worth pursuing, but it will only come to those who will do whatever it takes to get it. Are you among those who are desperate for more? Cry out from deep within, my precious friend: **"Draw me, we will run after thee: the king hath brought me into his chambers: we will be glad and rejoice in thee, we will remember thy love more than wine: the upright love thee."**

Take me by the hands. Walk toward me now, my Bridegroom! I hear the winds of change blowing; I hear the ring of visitation from my High Priest. You have entered the building ... you approach me now. You announce your presence... I am ready for my hour of visitation. Please, Beautiful One, do not come for only a visit but stay and dwell with me. Draw me! I treasure you! I cherish you! I need you forever and always! Amen!

Special Note to Our Readers:

Stay tuned for the sequel to this book. For we believe this is just an introduction to the message of the Bride and the Song of Solomon. Watch our website for details in the future. www.findrefuge.tv

ABOUT THE AUTHOR

Refuge Ministries

Steve and his wife Diane founded Refuge Ministries. Steve is a regular contributor to many prophetic publications including *The Elijah List, Spirit Fuel, and the Identity Network*. His writings have been read worldwide by hundreds of thousands of people. He also has been interviewed by the Trinity Broadcasting Network and a few other TV programs. Steve's books, articles, and videos have touched countless lives around the world. The Porters reside near Rochester, NY.

Dear Reader,

If your life was touched while reading *Draw Me-The Deep Cry of the Bride* please let us know! We would love to celebrate with you! Please visit our website, www.findrefuge.tv

Consumed by His Presence,

Steve Porter

♥

Draw Me

<u>**More Books by Steve & Diane Porter**</u>

Garden of The Heart- *Healing Letters to Ladies (Diane Porter)*

Crocodile Meat- *New and Extended Version (Steve's Life Story)*

Crocodile Meat- *Student Version*

Whispers from the Throne Room- *Reflections on the Manifest Presence*

Limitless

He Leads Me Beside Still Waters- *50 Love Letters of Healing and Restoration from Our Lord*

Streams in the Desert- *Healing Letters for the Wounded Heart*

Invading the Darkness- *Power Evangelism Training 101*

Pearls of His Presence- *Intimate Devotions for the Spiritually Hungry*

The Tongue of the Learned- *How to flow in the prophetic anointing*

Draw Me- *The Deep Cry of the Bride*

+ More!

Steve Porter

Coming in 2018 by Steve & Diane Porter

Hidden Treasure- *Intimate Devotions for the Spiritually Hungry*

Prayers of the Heart- *Intimate Prayers from a Love-struck Bride*

His Hands Extended- Stories of Love at the Nursing Home (Diane Porter)

For more info see our website

*Bulk orders and international orders are available upon request. Email for details.

www.findrefuge.tv

"Making your book dream come true without robbing you!"

www.deeperlifepress.com

Draw Me

New Books by Deeper Life Press

***Busyness*-** *The Greatest Threat to the Church Today*

By Bill Dick

***Catapulted*-** *Skillfully Navigating the Process of Your Journey*

By Joe Garcia

***The Glory Train*-** *Glory Revival Is Coming to the Nations!*

By Darren Canning

***A Life of Miracles*-** *My Supernatural Journey*

By Dr. Holly L. Noe

***Everyday Miracles*-** *Sixty-Four Stories of God's Love and Power*

By Sherry Evans

***Walter Beuttler*-** *My Spiritual Journey*

***Stepping Stones*-** *A Pathway into His Presence*

By Ryan Miller

Do you have a book in you? NO ONE beats our prices for the value—NO ONE! See the Deeper Life Press website for more!

www.deeperlifepress.com

P.O Box 1094

Canandaigua, NY 14424

www.findrefuge.tv

Rescue. Restore. Revive